The Tears of Mary -- and Fatima
Why?

"Return to my Son!"

by

ALBERT J. HEBERT, S.M.

An account, in the main, of Mary — and of her Son — as witnessed in her apparitions in recent times, as spoken of by her, and in particular as vicariously shed by her images, especially by her Fatima images; with some mention of stigmatists; and with some striking photos.

THE TEARS OF MARY—AND FATIMA

"Return to my Son!"

Dedicated

to

"THE WOMAN CLOTHED WITH THE SUN"

Who with her Son

will crush the Serpent

and bring the era of peace

promised

by

HER IMMACULATE HEART

at

FATIMA

Other books by the same author:

MARY OUR BLESSED LADY (72 Marian poems)
A CHRIST-FILLED WORLD (100 poems)
PRIESTLY CELIBACY: RECURRENT BATTLE AND
LASTING VALUES
MARY OUR BLESSED MOTHER
(96 Marian poems; Fatima statue tear photos)

NIHIL OBSTAT:
The Reverend Francis X. Kane, S.M., S.T.L.
Censor Deputatus

IMPRIMI PROTEST:
The Very Reverend Donald A. Romito, S.M., Ph.D.
Provincialis

NIHIL OBSTAT:
The Reverend Emanuel Camilleri, O.P., S.T.D., P.G.
Censor Deputatus

IMPRIMATUR:
The Most Reverend Stanley Joseph Ott, S.T.D., D.D.
Bishop of Baton Rouge

The *Nihil Obstat* and *Imprimatur* are official declarations that a book is free of doctrinal or moral error. No implication is contained therein that those who have granted the *Nihil Obstat* and *Imprimatur* agree with the contents, opinions, or statements expressed.

In no case does the *Nihil Obstat* and *Imprimatur* constitute an approval of any private revelations, prophecies, or possible new, incipient devotions or cults connected therewith, where they have not as yet been officially approved by the Church. Where such are treated as accounts in history or are reviewed in a reportorial manner as news of the day, the reader may always form his or her honest opinion or judgment according to the facts presented, spiritual guidance and wholesome discernment. That personal judgment, however, must be ready to respect the judgment of the Church when and if given, and at the place or source the instructions of the local Ordinary should be obeyed.

Regarding holiness of individuals, miracles, or other supernatural matters, the author in no wise presumes to anticipate judgments of the Church. In conformity with the Decree of Pope Urban VIII, purely human credibility applies to such narrations in this book.

ACKNOWLEDGMENTS:

The author desires to thank, first of all, those special souls, apparent genuine instruments of God, already departed from this life or still living, who have made possible a good part of this book. When it comes to weeping or bleeding images, he can only thank Christ and Our Lady. He also thanks all those who have encouraged the writing of this book and who have given helpful suggestions. And those who have provided photos and affidavits.

While the Bibliography gives a number of sources the author wishes to express thanks especially to *Divine Love* magazine. Fresno, CA. and *The Incredible Life Story of Sister Elena Aiello* (Spadafora—Cioffi. Theo Gaus, Inc., Brooklyn) for matter concerning the Calabrian Holy Nun. To the Blue Army, *Soul* magazine and Ave Maria Institute for helpful information (the latter for *The Angels* by Rev. Bede Dahmus, concerning Magdalen of the Cross). To the proper party for quotations concerning "Our Lady of America". To the publisher of the pamphlet. "Flame of Love" concerning the Hungarian mother and to Tan Publishers and the book, *Père Lamy* by Comte Paul Biver.

Finally for permission for quotations from two recent books, my thanks to: Edns. Resiac, 53150 Montsours, France, *Prophecies of La Fraudais,* Pierre Roberdel (Les Editions Saint-Raphael, Inc., Sherbrooke, Quebec, Canada, Jlh 1N5) and to Christopher Pub. House, West Hanover, MA., *Call of the Virgin at San Damiano* by Johan Osee.

Further, to St. Raphael Editions, Sherbrooke, for permission for quotations from *The Road That Leads to Life . . .* (Gaby's Diary) by Rev. J. A. Lamarche.

POSSIBLE SUGGESTION: Some readers may find the Preface chapter a bit "heavy" because it endeavors to clarify theologically some matters concerning private revelations. apparitions and the miraculous. If so, the reader might begin with the brief "Note to Readers" before the first chapter (I) and perhaps return later with more interest to this very important Preface.

CONTENTS

Preface

This author happily professes an unswerving loyalty to the Holy See, to Pope John Paul II and his teaching and to Holy Mother Church. Yet, to clear the air regarding private revelations, of which many have been reported in recent years, a few remarks might be opportune right at the beginning.

To begin with, we might ask a question with Father A. Poulain, S.J., probably the greatest modern authority on mystical theology: "Can we ever be *morally certain* that a revelation is purely *divine?*" Fr. Poulain answers: "Yes; although when we think of all the causes of error that have been enumerated it would not appear to be so."[1]

We know, however, that no Catholic is obligated by the Church to believe in any private revelation — except the convinced recipients of them — even those private revelations as famous as the ones reported of Lourdes and Fatima. The simple reason is that private revelations, of which there have been a large number in twenty centuries of Catholicism, do not constitute part of the original Deposit of Faith, the official Public Revelation of the Church which was closed out with the death of the last of the Apostles, Saint John the Evangelist.

The eminent and saintly Father R. Garrigou-Lagrange, O.P., in his *Three Ages of the Interior Life,* makes a good summary:

> "Divine revelations manifest supernaturally a hidden truth by means of a vision, a word, or only a prophetic instinct; they presuppose the gift of prophecy. They are called public if they have been made by the prophets, Christ, or the apostles, and are proposed to all by the Church, which preserves them in Scripture and tradition. They are called private when they are directed only to the particular benefit of certain persons. Private revelations, no matter what their importance, do not belong to the deposit of Catholic faith. However, some may draw attention to a certain form of worship of a nature to interest all the faithful, for example, the devotion of the Sacred Heart."[2]

Dogmas and truths pertinent to that original Deposit of Faith and Public Revelation are taught — or should be taught — in the regular catechetical works authorized by the Church Teaching, *Ecclesia Docens,* through the official Magisterium. We must allow room for the authentic development of dogma encased in that Deposit. So we have the Supremacy and Infallibility of the Pope clearly defined in Vatican I and the Immaculate Conception defined in 1854.

As an example of what Father Garrigou-Lagrange is referring to in the latter part of the above quotation, the definition of the Immaculate Conception was probably encouraged or hurried along by the Medal of the

Immaculate Conception apparition at Paris in 1830. Because of the many wonders connected with it the medal was subsequently called "The Miraculous Medal".

As only the principal teachings of the Church are summarized in catechisms, not a few Catholics are unaware of the many private revelations which have occurred throughout the ages. There are Catholics today who have never heard of the Fatima apparitions of 1917, nor of the Marian apparitions at LaSalette, France, 1846, Knock, Ireland, 1879, Beauraing, 1932-3 and Banneux, 1933, the latter two in Belgium; and others.

We should make a distinction between the person receiving a private divine revelation and the majority of people in the Church who are not the recipients of such but are aware of the claim made. Practically speaking we have a number of living claimants to private divine revelations and a good number of living persons intimately associated with them, the alleged privileged recipients. What then does the recipient have to believe and what about other Catholics?

As Father Poulain says: "when He so wills, God can give a complete certainty, while the revelation lasts, at any rate, to the person *receiving it*. The light and the evidence are of such strength that any kind of doubt is impossible. A similar fact occurs in the natural order. Our senses are subject to many illusions. But it is none the less true that in a multitude of cases we feel that we cannot have been mistaken."[3]

To further quote Fr. Garrigou-Lagrange:

> "According to certain theologians, a person who receives a private divine revelation with the certitude of its divine origin, like St. Joan of Arc, should believe in it with divine theological faith, for, in their opinion, the revelation contains the formal motive of infused faith, the authority of God revealing.
>
> "According to other theologians, and their opinion seems more exact, anyone who receives a certain private revelation should adhere to it immediately, not through divine faith but by prophetic light. This supernatural certitude may last, or on the contrary, give way to a moral certitude when the prophetic illumination disappears; but this illumination may return in order to restore the first certitude."[4]

Father Karl Rahner speaks of: "private revelations recommending a particular devotion, exhorting to penance, giving certain instructions, warning against certain doctrines, recommending a spiritual doctrine or manner of life, and so forth." Then he adds: "Without any doubt, in the course of the Church's history there have continually been private revelations of this kind, and they have exercised great influence."[5]

From the above assertions it can be seen that a very heavy burden of belief weighs upon recipients of private divine revelations. Consequently, Church authorities should treat claimants of such revelations with much circumspection and discernment, not to say, consideration, charity and care.

The Church, however, when it approves private revelations made to saints, holy persons or others, does not make an infallible pronouncement. The Church merely declares that the private revelations contain nothing contrary to Sacred Scripture and to Catholic teaching and, as Father Garrigou-Lagrange above continues, that they may be proposed as "probable to the pious belief of the faithful." What then when a Catholic has been exposed to the complete story of a Lourdes or Fatima? And/or when miracles or prophecies associated with private revelations are well established?

> As Fr. Poulain states: "When a *miracle* is performed, and it is stated that it is worked with this intention, or when circumstances show this to be the case, it is an undeniable proof of the divine nature of the revelation. A prophecy fulfilled, will be the equivalent of a miracle if it was couched in definite language and could not have been the result of chance or a conjecture of the Devil."[6]

One cannot deny his or her reason when faced with incontestable facts. How can one get around the announced apparition dates at Lourdes and Fatima, the miraculous spring at Lourdes and the spinning sun miracle at Fatima? Or the cures at both shrines? Would one off-handedly reject a private revelation which has received the commendation which accrues to shrines by reason of visits by Papel Legates (usually Cardinals) or the Popes themselves? Does not the presence of many Bishops, members of the clergy and religious orders, of deceased or living "saints" and of vast multitudes of pious faithful even to the millions have much weight? Does not the presentation of the Papal Golden Rose (as Pope Paul VI gave to the Shrine of Fatima), or a special statue crowning ceremony ordered by a Pope for one of these Shrines have some value?

It is evident then that where sufficient signs exist private revelations may be accepted by the general Catholic public on human faith, if also with prudence and without superstition. Further, no one should disdain or cast contempt on private revelations in general and especially where the Church has officially approved specific ones.

The approval of a private revelation by the Church as probable and worthy of pious belief does not mean that some error, personal attribution or false interpretation, especially in lengthy revelations, may not have slipped in. Even in such a case one can depend upon the *substance* of the revelation.

Some private revelations have achieved the purpose of their existence, i.e., the promulgation of a specific doctrine, despite the opposition raised against the revelations by some church authorities. Others successfully led to the establishment of a monastery or the founding of a religious order.

When St. Margaret Mary Alacoque received her revelations, 1673-75, with the instruction that she was to be the chosen instrument for spreading devotion to the Sacred Heart of Jesus, she was rebuffed by her superior, Mother de Saumaise, and unable to convince a group of theologians of the authenticity of her revelations. Blessed Claude dé la Colombière, however, her confessor believed the revelations to be genuine, but it took about ten years for her own community to turn around.

Any number of cases could be given regarding private revelations, where a few or many in opposition have been wrong and the one, two or three right. Take founders of religious orders: Francis of Assisi had visions leading to his life work and Jane Frances de Chantal one of her future director, Francis de Sales.

It would appear, however, that not all private revelations achieve their stated purpose. It would seem that some suffer so much harassment, interference and opposition from various sources, including ecclesiastical, that it is reasonable to believe that Christ or Mary will lessen the benefits in such cases, withdraw their own activity and influence at the site, and terminate the mission. This author could mention several such cases in the nineteenth and twentieth centuries where such sequences may have happened, but there is no point into getting into controversy here.

One might point out, however, that there have been similar cases in the Church which involved the teaching of truths necessary for salvation. For instance, Our Lord instructed the Apostles, where a city or a town would not receive them, to shake the dust off from their sandals and to go elsewhere. Christ used strong words, even terrifying words, to the effect that wicked cities like Sodom and Gomorrah would fare better on Judgment Day than those who were offered His truth and rejected it.

So, too, Saints Paul and Barnabas left troublesome Jews with the assertion that they, the Apostles, were turning to the Gentiles. Many later apostolic saints had similar experiences such as Francis of Assisi failing in his mission to the Moslems. But Francis was authentic. Paul and Barnabas were authentic.

It would seem that any good Catholic would give, with considered and balanced prudence, a most cordial welcome to any apparent instrument of God. It is unwise to take a preconceived, biased attitude in dealing with a possible instrument of God. If the works of God and unusual gifts of

Christ or Mary enter within our sphere of life or responsibility, we should be very cautious about taking the risk of throwing such works or signs back in the faces of Jesus and Mary, as it were, with pious excuses or unsubstantiated denouncements.

It is not our intention to judge any individual's motives. However, there have been persons, even ecclesiastics, who in all sincerity, indeed zealous sincerity, have meant well, but lacking full knowledge, practical investigating abilities, and/or courage, or all these qualities, have caused great loss of graces and other supernatural favors to the People of God.

An example: Our Lady af Fatima was so displeased with the harassment meted out to the child seers by the civil authority that she worked a lesser miracle (miracle of the sun, October 13, 1917) for a crowd of 70,000 or more. She herself declared on August 19, 1917, that a lesser miracle would be performed than originally intended. "If they had not taken you to the town (Ourem), the miracle would be even greater."

Another example: To spare his name, a certain cardinal in Europe at one time forbade his priests to go to Fatima under pain of excommunication. There are similar instances of restraint in the history of genuine apparitions, stigmatists, saints, seers and/or holy persons.

In matters of discipline neither do bishop-ordinaries or popes always make the wisest decisions though they may seem the best at the time. Such decisions not affecting faith or morals are reversible. So, while other popes had held otherwise, Saint Pius X changed the former discipline on the reception of Holy Communion and allowed little children to receive. In another area, although he was endowed with unusual mystical gifts and the stigmata, and received supernatural favors, the saintly Capuchin friar, Padre Pio, was restricted by the Holy See for about ten years from saying Mass publicly or seeing the people.

In earlier years Saint Joan of Arc was charged with heresy and witchcraft before the ecclesiastical court of Bishop Pierre Cauchon, her visions declared of diabolical origin, and, she was burned at the stake at Rouen on May 30, 1431. Pope Callistus III later appointed a court that found Joan innocent in 1456 and she was canonized in 1920. In our own days the private revelations of Sister Faustina of Poland were kept under wraps for years and her "Mercy of God" message and cult only approved (as she had foretold that it would be so later) when the present Polish Pope, John Paul II came into office.

In the cases of Padre Pio and Sister Faustina what could many good people surmise for years but that Rome or the Congregation there in charge must be right and Padre Pio and Sister Faustina not authentic? Padre Pio obeyed and Sister Faustina was submissive to God's permissive will. The world-wide supporters of Sister Faustina also submitted. They stored away tremendous amounts of "Mercy of God" devotional literature and holy pictures. Now the life, private revelations, diary and apparitions to Sister Faustina are being spread all over the world.

If the local Ordinary had restricted Padre Pio, the Capuchin friar — though holy persons rarely do so — might have appealed to the Pope. But where does one appeal when convinced he has an authentic mission and the popes themselves have acted negatively in the case? When Padre Pio submitted he wept, not on the restrictions placed on himself — an isolated life would be easier for him as a contemplative religious — but for all the graces that would be lost to the people.

We have seen the burden an authentic private revelation places on the convinced recipient, especially where there is unbelief, contradictions, harassment and even persecution on the part of others. As Rahner says ". . . the theologians normally concede that the immediate recipient of a private revelation can and even (given sufficient certitude) must believe it *fide divina . . .*"[7] That is, with divine faith but not Catholic Faith as with respect to Public Revelation. It would seem that a learned, holy and prudent spiritual director and/or confessor of the recipient would almost be of a belief similar to that of the recipient. Prescinding from these intimates, what of the general Catholic Faithful?

What are the rights of individuals, who are convinced of the authenticity of a certain private revelation and mission of the claimant recipient, and who then learn that the local Ordinary has given out a statement to the effect that nothing "supernatural" has occurred, or there is no reason for such belief? In such a case a better informed bishop elsewhere (as happens), a mystical theologian close to the "seer", a well-informed priest or layman may simply respond:

"The Church does not oblige me to accept a judgment as *true* when a local ordinary, as at Beauraing or Banneux, declares a particular revelation to be credible. That is because it is not a matter of divine Catholic Faith, and in this area, that of private revelations, the judgment of the Bishop-Ordinary is not objectively infallible.

"Conversely, I do not have to accept a negative or condemnatory statement from a bishop in the case of a private revelation, especially when I have had close contact with the principals or have acquired extensive knowledge of the matter through competent witnesses, authors, priests, theologians and other professional people, and have reached a considered judgment adverse to that of the local Ordinary. I cannot deny my reason and the facts, the truth where I believe the local bishop to be wrong in this case, anymore than I can take the risk of denying a long and well-established private revelation, such as that made at Lourdes, with all its documentation, to be true."

It is possible that there are some shrines in the long history of the Church that have grown famous when there was actually *no* authentic apparition as claimed. And there can be miracles happening there because of the good faith of the people. It is also possible that some sites of genuine apparitions and private revelations have been injudiciously opposed and suppressed. Only God knows!

In a word, if a Catholic is free to disbelieve what a particular Ordinary states is credible, then also an informed Catholic can personally believe in a particular private revelation, which another particular Ordinary declares is not worthy of human credence. (We speak here, of course strictly of private revelations, not of any matter of faith or morals associated with a revelation.)

So, it is possible for Catholics, in these matters, to accept a certain judgment as valid and to deny another as authentic, privately, personally, not speaking for the Church. Fundamentally a private revelation remains a matter of human credibility for the individual in relation to the experience of that person with regard to an alleged supernatural manifestation.

What then should be the position of the good, competent Catholic, especially one experienced in "mystical" matters or with professional knowledge, who is convinced of the authenticity, at least in substance, of a private revelation, when the local Ordinary gives a negative judgment?

The first thing to do is to respect both the Bishop and his episcopal office and to avoid giving any scandal. This applies especially to those persons in his diocese and subject to his authority and direction. Any Catholic, however, also has to protect his own God-given integrity, loyalty to the truth, and even to the good of the Church. Again I say, where *competent* and *well-informed* persons are concerned one cannot dodge life and the responsibilities that come with a confrontation of truth.

If a Catholic dwells in the same diocese where the apparently debatable episcopal decision or decree has been made, then he or she has practical problems. One hesitates to gainsay openly the expressed declaration of one's bishop. Prudence and patient suffering may be combined here and a refraining from any belligerent public statements. Understanding might be reached for the expression of one's own reasoned opinion backed up by facts. But there should be no coercion affecting one's *private* convictions or the holding and communication of them. Persons with such convictions should not be treated as if they were denying truths of the Faith. (It is something else if they are promoting a *new*, unauthorized cult in the diocese).

The reasons for one's convictions, and evidence such as privately secured statements, photos, affidavits, professional conclusions, can be privately submitted to the Bishop himself and should be received by him with appreciation and open mind. (And I would stress "to the bishop", because there have been chancery officials who have acted on their own or left ordinaries not fully informed.) Such respectful cooperation can be helpful to the Church.

We must stress here that a number of prelates have certainly taken their obligations and duties in these matters very seriously. That is why we have so many authorized Marian shrines in the past century and a half alone.

In the case of restrictive commands issued by the local Ordinary the position of the seer/s can be made very distressful. This is especially true where no matter of faith or morals is in question, and where, on the contrary, there are only exhortations to hold on to orthodox doctrine and to practice traditional devotions; and where there is no public preaching of or liturgical ceremonies involving any new authorized cult.

No doubt, wisely or not, the local bishop can control or forbid the celebration of Mass at the site (or home) of alleged apparitions or private revelations, and also control any official liturgical devotion, the reservation of the Blessed Sacrament, etc. Today, however, we have this strange phenomenon, that at many charismatic group meetings Mass is offered on the same occasion and site, when and where, "praying in tongues", "words of knowledge", "prophecies", "healing" and "cures" are claimed, and without any episcopal comment or investigation. Yet, certain restricted "seers", apparently genuine mystics and instruments of God, have had much more striking supernatural "credibilia", as believed by competent witnesses, and have been limited in their activities in seemingly unreasonable ways and for trying periods of time. (This is not to put down the many authentic charismatic gifts among Catholics today.)

In the present disciplinary attitude of the Church it seems that no Ordinary can forbid prayer gatherings, simple prayer vigils, etc., at the site of alleged private revelations and apparitions. By a decree of the Sacred Congregation for the Doctrine of the Faith approved October 14, 1966 by Pope Paul VI, Canons 1399 and 2318 were abrogated. This decree went into effect March 29, 1967. On November 15, 1966, the above Congregation answered a question concerning the decree.

"Question: Whether Canon 1399 by which certain books are forbidden *ipso jure,* and Canon 2318 by which certain penalties are decreed against those who violate laws concerning the censure and prohibition of books remain in effect."

"Reply: 1. In the negative to both, as regards the force of ecclesiastical law; inculcating again, however, the validity of the moral law, which completely prohibits the endangering of faith and morals." The decree was signed by A. Cardinal Ottaviani as Pro-prefect and P. Parente as Secretary of the Congregation. (See *AAS*-58-1186 & *Canon Law Digest,* Vol. 6, p. 814).

In a word there is much freedom today in propagating alleged revelations, visions, prophecies and miracles. It is also interpreted that it is permitted to all Catholics to visit places of apparitions, even those not recognized as such by the local Ordinaries of the dioceses or by the Pope. (Rome usually follows the approval of a local Ordinary; or a Roman Congregation will state the fact of an unfavorable declaration made by a local Ordinary.)

It would seem then that wise ordinaries would be careful not to issue negative or condemnatory statements or restrictions, especially where there is no proven fraud or offense to Catholic doctrine, morals or liturgy. Again, if any statement is issued in a negative manner, such should come only after a thorough canonical investigation, with interviews held with all the principals free from duress and pressure, and with the many other usual competent witnesses available. A one-sided leaning to prejudiced or "opposition" witnesses should be avoided. The same for all official investigation personnel!

If such a commission or diocesan tribunal gives a negative report which is adopted by the Bishop, such a report like one stating that he sees no reason to believe anything of a supernatural nature has occurred or it all can be explained "naturally", then surely some rationale and proof for such a general statement should be offered mature and intelligent Catholics and the world at large.

This would seem to apply in particular when many competent priests (even bishops from other areas), professional experts and ordinary competent laity witness to what they judge supernatural elements, such as ecstasy, levitation, unusual knowledge displayed, "cures", prophecies fulfilled, spiritual conversions, and great improvement in religious life, personal, communal and beyond. (This author is aware of some very holy and/or responsible Catholics, including bishops and holy priests who have convictions at odds with certain negative judgments of ecclesiastics made concerning alleged private revelations occurring in our times — and the author does not mean Necedah nor Bayside.)

Prudent prelates will know how to make contingent statements until the matter of a private revelation is finally and definitively settled. Sometimes the best action is to let it run its course without interference and not to deny priests, for example, access to seer/s. Where indeed would many seers of the past and of our own times have been, saints even, if denied some good priests to objectively but kindly judge them; and to console and comfort them in very trying circumstances, especially in hard trials directly stemming from criticism, condemnation and even persecution by certain clerics?

Indeed, it could be very helpful to an Ordinary if he judiciously encouraged his priests and those of other dioceses to prudently and kindly visit such sites and seers, and, afterwards to privately report any observations and convictions. He would be much better informed then and in a better position for making judgments.

It happens at times that certain chancery officials when interviewed or queried give out their own preconceived or prejudicial views instead of a set diocesan position, if there is one. It happens also that very competent priests from other dioceses or countries visit seers or apparition sites and may be better qualified professionally than anyone in a local diocese in such matters. An open-minded ordinary could learn much from inviting such priests or other visiting professionally qualified persons to brief him on their findings. After all it is one holy Catholic Church!

It is a heavy responsibility and risk to forbid priests to visit such sites or seers. Great good has come to many priests from contacts with such chosen instruments of God, at times with persons later to become canonized saints of God. It is hard to see where any evil has come from such visits.

We hear at times that priests have been forbidden to visit an apparition site or a priest has been "silenced" because "the priest represents the Church and the people will think the Church has given approval." The priest, as we have seen above, has the right to his individual convictions in the above matters. The people know well that he does not speak for the Church — or they can be told so — and that it is the Bishop who will give the "final" judgment. If an individual priest claims he is speaking for the Church or claims the Church has given a judgment when it has not, it is a simple matter for the Bishop to instruct the people properly.

An anticipation, however, of what might happen in an individual case should not prejudice the rights and good of many priests and other persons. As we have indicated, some chancery officials speak out as if they were the Bishop. They too stand correction! If anything, they should be neutral until a decree has been issued. A definitive decree!

It will be noted by persons knowledgeable about current claims that this author in this book does not treat of several alleged private revelations about which there has been much publicity. He omits such, in two cases at least, because, for one thing, the two separate "seers" involved have been singled out by their Bishop-Ordinaries as "disobedient". As observed above — and prescinding from the just mentioned two instances — even when seemingly harsh or unjust restrictions are imposed, good "seers" obey them as best they can interpret them. Rarely if ever do they appeal to any higher ecclesiastical authority.

In addition, if such "seers" have spiritual directors, which they should, good spiritual directors would advise them to obey, pray and be patient. Too many persons today, including some theologians make the mistake of trying to work outside the hierarchial structure of the Church. (It should be noted here that any "seer" or privileged soul should be free to seek a spiritual director of his or her own choice or be able to give personal assent to any appointee. Further, they should be free to choose another director when a director is found to be incompetent. The great St. Teresa of Avila pointed out the difficulties she experienced in seeking good spiritual directors. Again, this author is aware of at least five persons worthy of credence as authentic instruments of God, who, in these United States, have found great difficulties in securing good spiritual directors. Such persons need much consideration, consolation and prayers).

Disobedience, even that of a genuine priest or an authentic seer is not a good sign. Recall, we have mentioned earlier that there can be a possible withdrawal of Christ or Mary from a genuine private revelation and the mission of a picked instrument, if there is sufficient interference or opposition. It is not within our province to make any specific judgments in particular cases, but simply to say in general that persons knowledgeable in these matters might surmise what might have happened in the cases of some apparently genuine "missions" — at least viable for a while — with their associated private revelations and supernatural manifestations.

We have said above "a genuine priest or an authentic seer". There are Catholics who think it a great privilege and wonder to witness a lame man walk, an image of Mary to weep or to have some seer prophesy in their presence. Yet these same Catholics take as routine happenings the daily consecration of bread and wine into the Body and Blood of Christ, the forgiveness of serious sin by the same priest or his frequent reading of prophetic Scripture. Yet many such priests with such real powers have given up their priesthood, especially in our days, and some their Catholic Faith. Such defections or apostasies did not invalidate the truly valid consecrations and absolutions of earlier, happier days.

So, too, as the priest is given wonderful supernatural gifts, powers for the good of the People of God, certain persons have been given special revelations and charismatic gifts for the benefit of the Church. Such *gratiae gratis datae* (graces freely given) like working wonders and cures, prophecy, discernment of spirits, etc., as Father John Arintero, O.P. says, "are directly ordained to the good of others,".[8] For instance, the Apostles, Judas along with them, went out on mission endowed with charismatic gifts. We can assume that Judas then cured people and drove out demons, perhaps even raised the dead. But let us turn from this extreme case.

Our Lord said, while on earth, that many would knock at heaven's door and demand entrance saying they had employed charismatic gifts in His Name. But His answer was, "I know you not!" — because they had failed in vital things. People can have had charismatic gifts at one time, and, whatever the cause/s, have failed. Priests have abandoned exercising supernatural gifts. Unfortunately there are persons in hell who once possessed chrismatic gifts. And there are priests in hell who once called down Christ upon the altar. These terrible facts only accent the need of charitable prayers for both priests and those given special gifts from God.

It is possible then that, because of human failure in once chosen instruments, Our Lord or Mary may withdraw from a mission, permanently, or perhaps for a time. Christ and Mary can move to other sites and other seers. Graces and gifts can be distributed in many other ways. God is not limited. And it may be just another parabolic illustration of, "Take his talent and give it to another!"

We have pointed out that there can be other "interference" (as one mystic known to the author calls it) with a mission: various kinds of pressure, harassment or opposition, even ecclesiastical neglect, strictures or persecution. Again, within the Church a "prophet" or saint has not been accepted in his own order or has been exiled from his own diocese, as a John of the Cross imprisoned by his fellow Carmelites or a founder, St. Alphonsus Liguori replaced as superior in his own congregation. Or take a St. Athanasius condemned by Emperor-packed councils of bishops, and a St. John Chrysostom condemned by 36 hostile bishops at the Synod of the Oak; or similarly treated St. Gregory of Nyssa — all Fathers and Doctors of the Church!

So, when it comes to chosen instruments, priesthood, religious or otherwise, some falter, some are faulted, some fail, others are "removed" or suppressed; some, it might be said, *some* die in the glory of possession or restoration, and for others glory only comes afterwards.

The reader, or some readers, will note that this author details nothing about Garabandal in the following chapters of this book. He is aware of negative *nota* or statements of several of its ordinaries (See of Santander). He also has read more than a half-dozen volumes with much documentation on Garabandal. He never "pushes" Garabandal. But it is his considered private opinion that in the first years there were many manifestations at Garabandal that in substance cannot be explained away as being merely natural. And there have been many good, competent priests, professional experts like doctors and other competent witnesses of similar opinion to buttress his own.

That the Garabandal case is permanently closed would be premature to assume. The present bishop of Garabandal, I understand, has been sympathetic and open-minded. A difficult matter for the Church, for one thing, has been the specific prophecies made at Garabandal. Warnings, chastisements, need of reparation, we hear of them from many sources. The televisable sign to remain at the Pines after the Great Miracle is understandably something neither Rome nor Santander care to go out on a limb with an endorsement. Yet Fatima had its own specific prophecies which continue to unfold many years later. Watch, wait, pray!

Soul magazine, Jan.-Feb. 1979, tells of Michael Servant's interview (in his book, *Watch and Pray*) with Cardinal Ottaviani in October 1970 about the 1960 Secret of Fatima: "On our insistence about the publication of the secret of Fatima possibly having something to do with the good of souls, the Cardinal answered: 'That which the Blessed Virgin wishes is prayer and penance. It is necessary to preach prayer and penance in order that if there is good in the secret it will come, and if there is bad, that it will not come.' "

It would seem, that whatever the mystery of Garabandal and its future, the above advice of the eminent Cardinal given with regard to the Secret of Fatima, is very applicable to a living of the exhortations of Garabandal to prayer and penance in reparational practices today.

Along these lines, at the end of this book one will find the basic Fatima revelations, prophecies and requests. To concentrate on the message of Fatima alone should be sufficient for most people, especially in view of the fact of so many *Fatima* images weeping tears in the past decade or so.

Finally the author has included in this volume as simple historical record, brief "tear" quotations from the San Damiano, Italy messages and the La Fraudais, France alleged private revelations. The author is not aware that either seer, Mama Rosa or Marie Jules Jahenny (deceased), both of whom experienced some negative judgments and rather harsh restrictions, ever disobeyed their Ordinaries. Obedience is always a good sign. So it is possible that time will prove them right. But we would have far more than enough accounts in the book without these two or many other seers we might adduce. The tears of Mary and Christ have splattered on this world and age in a manner no one can escape.

"I drench my couch with my tears." Ps. 6:7.

A NOTE FROM THE AUTHOR TO READERS

It is important for readers to note here and to remember in the reading of this book, that our subject does not concern the detailing of lengthy private revelations, messages and other apparent supernatural phenomena often connected with individuals mentioned in this book. We are largely limited to a consideration of *tears*, mainly the "tears" of Mary and her Son Jesus, as wept vicariously through their images.

We also note cases where privileged souls tell of their witnessing Mary crying or Christ bleeding in apparitions. Further, we point out where Jesus and Mary in apparitions tell of their own tears or sorrows. Additionally, we bring in a few stigmatists who are examples of Catholics sharing in Christ's bleedings in a special manner.

This treatment of themes in the book may seem "negative" to some and full of suffering and sorrow. It is not negative and is meant to be striking and soul-arresting. Salvation comes through suffering and the Cross.

The book would have to be enlarged endlessly to consider but briefly the many hopeful promises and cheering messages that also go with the reported private revelations, along with those calling for much seriousness, sorrow, redemptive suffering and tears. Many more instances of the patience, forgiveness, mercy and love of God for mankind could be brought out than are mentioned in this book. Christ and Mary often speak of or allude to the kindness, compassion, love, mercy, forgiveness and helpfulness of God for all.

Again, there is the undoubted eventual triumph of good over evil and the coming victory of the Immaculate Heart of Mary. Such encouraging elements are endless in modern manifestations and private communications of Christ and Mary to victim souls and chosen instruments.

The author believes that the authentic accounts of tears along with limited references to messages considered authentic by many persons will lead readers to seek and discover the spiritual riches awaiting them in many individual and fuller works such as those listed in the bibliography. The concrete factors of many vicarious tears presented through numerous images of Christ and Mary surely will move many persons to search out and contemplate the far bigger picture, that is, the whole worldwide and complete story of God's Mercy, Love and Providence for the human family.

Hopefully this book will also lead to another volume with a fuller treatment of apparent supernatural communications, private revelations and other unusual phenomena that back up and make urgent the living-out of the spiritual requests so often made by Our Lord and His Blessed Mother in our days.

The overall message is always that of a needed response to the appeal of a Saviour's sorrowing and a Mother's shedding of tears. Mercy and love are always held out to those intent on a genuine renewal of Christian life and with a sincere will to make generous reparation.

In the end Christ and the Immaculate Heart of His Holy Mother will triumph completely, crushing the serpent's evil head and frustrating his poisonous fangs. It is up to us to triumph with them and to help others participate in that victory. But the road to Easter and Resurrection is through the paths of suffering and the Way of the Cross, of prayer and reparation for others. Easter Sunday is beyond Calvary and Good Friday. But Easter Sunday always comes. We believe a real big one is coming before long. We also believe there is going to be a big Holy Week before it!

> "Yes, precisely. If men do not correspond there will be more suffering. But the victory of the Immaculate Heart of Mary will come because She has promised this." Sister Lucia of Fatima, as reported by John Haffert in *Soul* magazine, Jul-Aug 1982.

Apparition, Our Lady at Zeitun (Cairo) Egypt

I — CHRIST AND MARY WEEP THROUGH IMAGES

"A cry was heard at Ramah, sobbing and loud lamentation:"

Mt. 2:18.

Copious tears of Mary were wept vicariously, through the image of her in Syracuse, Sicily, for four days in 1953. Much earlier Our Lady in a personal apparition wept at the dry stream bed at La Salette, France, in 1846, where she appeared to Melanie and Maximin.

Mary also shed tears "personally" when consoling the Belgian mystic, Berthe Petit, in her, the latter's sufferings in March, 1938.

In the spring of 1973 a Head of Christ, a replica of that of the Olimpias (Spain) gushed tears in a small town in the State of New York. (Name of the place is omitted to protect privacy.) The image also shed blood on Good Friday of 1973 and 1974.

Years before that, 1893-4, tears flowed from the eyes of Mary in a *Pieta* image belonging to the holy Flemish Benedictine, Father Paul of Moll, in Flanders, Europe (Abbey of Termonde or nearby area).

An International Pilgrim Virgin Fatima statue — the "European" one — of the Blue Army wept at Las Vegas, Nevada, before its world traveling Peace tour in 1978. The same International Pilgrim Virgin statue wept in Carthage, N.Y., May 7, 1980.

A much more famous weeping was that of the official, original 1947 International Pilgrim Virgin Fatima statue to North America which occurred at New Orleans on Monday and Tuesday, July 17, 18, 1972. More, the same famous statue wept again a few days later in Atlanta, July 21, and finally in New York State in a small town ("c") on August 5, 1972.

In the life of the holy priest, Pére Lamy of France (1855-1931), by Comte Paul Biver, we learn of an image of Mary, a statue weeping in his garden.

Teresa Musco is a recently deceased (1976) stigmatist as dependable reports, literature and photos testify. In her home at Caserta, not far from Rome, images of Christ and Mary wept, shed blood, or both in 1976, before her death, including images of the *Bambino* and Our Lady of Fatima. (See life, *Teresa Musco, "Crocifissa col Crocifisso"*, replete with many photos.) Teresa's cause for canonization is already under way.

Do these various reports seem incredible or exaggerated? Know then, there is an entire book, *Segno Dei Tempi?—Signs of the Times?*— (with photos) concerning sacred images weeping in Italy alone in recent decades, including bloody images of Christ and Mary. In Italy alone, we repeat, there is a whole book on weeping images and reputed Marian apparitions there. Apparitions may be hard to prove by themselves alone. Tears of salt taste and of blood recorded on cameras, and analyzed in laboratories as such, are more "objective".

The Blessed Mother in certain well regarded private revelations has spoken of her tears shed through some of these images. For instance, in the book, *Our Lady Speaks to Her Beloved Priests*, Mary speaks to Don Stephano Gobbi, privileged priest instrument of the Marian Movement of Priests: "Never before, as in these times, has your heavenly Mother been so concerned, I might even say anguished. I draw close to the hearts of My beloved sons.

"I am pleading with you through manifestations that are becoming more numerous and more evident. My tears, my apparitions, my messages." (Jan. 21, 1978)

Have you heard of an Immaculate Conception Lady of Lourdes statue that wept several times in 1972? In or about a small town in New York State. Or another famous Fatima statue of a certain lady that has been estimated as weeping over 50 times since 1972, including local and other well-known weepings on Long Island? (No reference to Bayside!) Do you know that this same Fatima statue wept in Washington, D.C., Pittsburgh, Chicago and other places? That, after the statue was "quiet" for sometime, it was weeping again in 1981? (For purposes of limited identification in this book we shall refer to the lady connected with these and other weeping images, pseudonymously, as "AW".)

Do you know that a National Fatima Pilgrim Virgin statue has wept in Syria?

Or that there have been many weepings of two other *Fatima* statues in New Orleans and its metropolitan area? (*Not* the original Pilgrim Virgin statue of 1972!) And weepings of other images there, including ones of Christ? And other reported weepings of other images in Louisiana?

But also of weepings of images in other places? Like a significantly entitled Marian statue in Madrid, Spain, bleeding from the eyes and heart? (As we shall see later.)

Yes, that in more than one of her statues Mary has bled, vicariously as it were, *from the heart*, her Immaculate Heart!

What does it all mean?

We shall give reportorial facts and readers can draw their own conclusions.

Perhaps a quotation from the Old Testament is apt here:

"Do not the tears that stream down her cheek cry out against him that causes them to fall?" (Sirach 35:15)

II — JESUS' TEARS, MARY'S SWORD OF SORROW

". . . in great sorrow and anguish, with copious tears . . ." **2 Cor. 2:4**

The tears of Jesus are not new. He wept at Lazarus' grave. He wept over Jerusalem. Such are Gospel accounts: " 'Where have you laid him?' They said to Him, 'Lord, come and see.' Jesus wept. So the Jews said, 'See how He loved him.' " (John 11:34-36)

Jesus still weeps today over a mankind He loves, a mankind which, to a great extent, is spiritually dead. Jesus also weeps over the good who are suffering severe hardships, who are being persecuted, and over some who are being martyred.

Jesus weeps over a world facing terrible tribulations and chastisements because of its sins, the errors and evils permeating and dominating it. His cry in Judea rings out again today, everywhere: "Jerusalem, Jerusalem, how often have I wanted to gather your children together as a mother bird collects her young, under her wings, and you refused Me!"

(Matt. 23:37)

Jesus weeps today over the Jerusalem that is the modern world, even over many people who are members of the New Jerusalem, His Holy Church. — Jesus wept! — and Jesus weeps!

"Look, Master, what wonderful stones and what wonderful buildings!"—so one of the disciples exclaimed on sighting the towering Temple buildings.

"And Jesus said to him. 'Do you see these great buildings? There will not be left here one stone upon another, that will not be thrown down.' " (Mark 13:1-2)

Weep, indeed, Jesus! The Jerusalem of this world is at the crossroads of history again today. Proud towers await their toppling down. The Arm of the Father's Justice hangs closely over them. And your Blessed Mother's arms are outstretched in pleading for additional mercy. Weep your own tears, Jesus, and weep over your Mother's tears.

For Mary, too, weeps, for it pleases Jesus to weep most through His Mother — and this is nothing new!

The New Testament writings do not say, directly, that the Mother of Sorrows wept. It is not necessary to say so—*stabat autem juxta crucem Jesu Mater Ejus!* "There stood by the cross of Jesus, His Mother." No doubt she wept there!

Of Mary it also was prophesied by the holy Simeon: "A sword will pass through your heart!" And the Church applies to that Sorrowing and

Immaculate Mother, the words: "O come all of you who pass along the way and see: Is there any sorrow like unto my sorrow?"

Does a Mother not share tears during such grief? Even in the very beginning of Jesus' life it was like that for Mary. As she fled to Egypt with the Child, the Bible records how Herod's murderous soldiers cruelly massacred the Holy Innocents — "A voice was heard in Ramah, wailing and loud lamentation, Rachel weeping for her children; she refused to be consoled, because they were no more." (Matt. 2:18)

Is it conceivable that Rachel, the ancestress of the slaughtered innocents of Bethlehem, figuratively wept over her descendent children, and that the Spiritual Mother of them all, Mary, did not? Or that the cries and sobs of the living mothers did not echo in Mary's ears a long time, on her exile road to Egypt, with a sympathetic flow of her own tears?

No one wept like Mary wept. No one weeps like Mary weeps today.

Mary weeps over the slaughter of million of the Innocents today, over the slaughter of bodies, but much more so over the slaughter of souls. She is hard put to hold back the wrath of her Just Son and Arm of His Just Father. Indeed it may well be a great mercy that Justice soon falls on the human race to finish off much evil, and to prevent its increasing propagation with more and more souls scandalized to their eternal ruin, and more and more of the young and the innocent betrayed.

A new handwriting is on the wall of the modern world-wide Babylon. As we shall see, it spells out these words: The Tears of Mary and Jesus, tears of salt, tears of blood, tears of sympathy and sadness, tears of anguish and sorrow. But, above all, they are tears of appeal lest the catastrophe of the Father's justice fall on the human race and the world in general; and many souls be eternally lost. A catastrophe of mercy, true, for some, but of annihilation, even everlasting desolation for others.

Let us begin to look at the Tears of Mary and Jesus, especially the plentiful tears of Mary. And perhaps to well up some of our own. First, however, let us consider miraculous sacred images in general.

> *"Se la Madonna piange, vuol dire che ci sono i motivi"* — "If the Madonna weeps, it asks the motives for it." Papa Giovanni Paolo II: 28-2-1979.

III — MIRACULOUS IMAGES

***"I will weep in secret many tears."* Jer. 13:17.**

The weeping of Christ and Mary, vicariously, through their images, like their personal crying while on earth, is not new in the Church. Speaking in general, there have always been miraculous images present in the history of the Church; and some have wept. Some have moved, have smiled, have bowed the head or changed expression.

But there never has been such an outpouring of tears as there has been in this century and in the past few decades, and, more explicitly, during the ten years, 1971-1981, particularly so in Italy and in the United States. The reader may begin to wonder, to surmise, to move toward some early conclusions as to what is behind all this: tears, and locale; and what the symbol, meaning, or "message".

Obviously, what is unique in history and set in a religious frame, must be of serious if not grave significance to mankind for whom the signs are intended. These numerous tears have not been wept over apes or apricots; or to move stones or trees to sympathetic sorrow and repentance.

There are always occurring many wonders concerning which we are never aware: some far away, some of local interest, and some that have been concerned primarily with individual persons. But where the miraculous or the supernatural makes an explosive entry into ordinary life, or the extraordinary becomes multiple, it cannot escape some prominent notice, significance and historical reality. It cannot be evaded!

In the Church many claims have been made for miraculous religious images of all sorts, crucifixes, pictures, statues of Christ or Mary, icons of all kinds, including those of the saints. We will look at a few of these "miraculous" images in general before pursuing our more limited field of *weeping* images that give a dramatic, and touching, if also silent but moving sign-language from those persons they represent.

First of all, the term "miraculous image" does not necessarily mean anything extraordinary or "supernatural" has occurred in the image itself. It often means that a certain image, say of Our Lady, under some specific title, is the center of much devotion to Mary. Before it prayers rise for help and intercession through Mary herself, for some favor, miracle or cure. Because many claims have been made for answers to such petitions the statue or image becomes known, even famous, as a "miraculous" one.

This does not mean that certain famous "miraculous images", say those of "Our Mother of Perpetual Help", "Our Lady of Lourdes", Saint

Jude, etc., have not been seen by some individuals to change expression, smile, weep, bow the head or shed a tear or two. Such an experience can truly have been granted to one person in a group as a personal spiritual favor, without others in the group experiencing it. When great numbers of pilgrims pray before such images daily for years, even for centuries, it is very probable that these types of happenings have occurred.

But, if we take less famous images, say, that of the statue of Our Lady of Prompt Succor, Patroness of Louisiana and New Orleans, in the Ursuline Convent in New Orleans, or that of Our Lady of Lourdes in the Grotto Chapel of Saint Michael's Church at Convent, La., or that of Saint Ann in her national shrine in New Orleans, though many favors are attributed to the patronesses or patrons of such shrines, one is not generally aware that any of these images have wept or exhibited other miraculous manifestations.

We would not deny, however, that they may be, or have been some persons who have had such individual "supernatural" experiences with those images. This author, in his lifetime, has had too many reliable confidences of such experiences related to him by balanced, responsible persons. He has also heard from certain people "religious experiences" he either rejects or doubts as genuine.

We are looking at "miraculous" images of the past to get a better appreciation of the authenticity and significance of the weeping images of our times, in our own days, indeed weeping at the very *hours* of writing this book.

Some "miraculous images" became so from long years of prayer before them. Some others became so when they began to manifest extraordinary or reasonably believed "supernatural" activities. Others were considered "miraculous" because of mysterious origins, such as being thrown up by the sea (like "Our Lady of Charity, Patroness of Cuba", 1625), or being led to, or retrieved, under unusual circumstances; or through private revelations (Our Lady of Pompeii picture; Le Puy, Pontmain, Lourdes).

Let us take from several such considerations perhaps the most unusual and most famous of all miraculous images, that of Our Lady of Guadalupe in the environs of Mexico City. When the simple Aztec, a Christian Indian, the peon, Juan Diego, opened his cloak or tilma in 1531 (450 years ago!), he thought he was presenting the sign for Bishop John Zumarraga of Mexico (1531), in the miraculous Castilian roses Mary had provided.

Mary had given them to Juan on the wintry, bare hill of Tepeyac with its soil and the season then unfavorable to such beautiful roses. Mary herself had arranged the flowers in Juan's cloak with her own discerning womanly hands.

But Bishop Zumarraga did not fall on his knees precipitately before miraculous roses, astounding and lovely as they were, fresh and fragrant from the Queen of Heaven. The bishop knelt in awe before perhaps the most unique miraculous image given to mankind in all history.

There before the Bishop, almost as if Mary herself was presenting the Castilian roses, was a most beautiful "painting" of rare colors. It was that of Mary herself, Our Lady of Guadalupe. It was impressed on or in poor cactus cloth that was nothing like the material of an oil canvass suitable for a great painting. More, subsequently, it should have disintegrated within a few decades, but it has endured into its fifth century.

I say, "unique" miraculous image because Mary herself presented this image of herself, whatever way it was instantaneously "painted" by herself, some angel, or heaven-dwelling saint.

It is true that we have the famed "Shroud of Turin", Our Lord's reputed burial cloth. I say "reputed", because, though its genuineness has many arguments for it, it would seem very hard if not impossible to definitely and historically establish it as such. Similarly for the reputed "Veil of Veronica".

If, however, these two holy objects, which have affected many persons spiritually for their good, are someday — and I certanly hope so — finally established as authentic, they would have a natural, if miraculously preserved, "base" in their being "normal" cloths that had an original contact with the Body and with the Holy Countenance of Jesus. That is to say, they are objective, human-made material cloths. Such holy contacts, however, would make them priceless relics of the utmost pre-eminence.

The miraculous image of Our Lady of Guadalupe, however, came, as it were, out of the blue sky from Mary, amid the snow-capped mountains near Mexico City, though actually bestowed by the hillside of Tepeyac. It is utterly miraculous in origin then and also in its preservation both from internal decay and external attack.

Concerning the latter, on November 24, 1921, a bomb was placed near the sacred image in the then great, old-shrine basilica. The force of the explosion twisted a large metal crucifix on the altar and did not harm the miraculous image, the "painting" of Mary.

That twisted crucifix is enclosed today in a heavy, ornamental but open-view glass repository. It is near the entrance to the escalators that carry pilgrims beneath the famous old painting in the new modern shrine.

ordained a priest May 8, 1983). A Baby Jesus image also became animated and told "Brother" Gino to hold a procession to alleviate local flood conditions. This author has been in the presence of such a fragrance from a famous Fatima statue ("AW's") placed in a convent chapel in Chicago. Others there also smelled it. The fragrance lingered for a day and more. And that happened in mid-winter when heavy snow lay all around.

It is not our purpose to inquire into or even list all older miraculous or weeping miraculous images. It is not our purpose either to burden the reader with endless citations for every given instance — books in the bibliography will back-up our presentations with more wonders than years of reading could handle. The author, however, wishes to point out a certain phenomenon. He has done much research in all areas of the "supernatural" and miraculous: cures, miracles, charismatic gifts, apparitions, visions, prophecies, stigmatists, seers, bilocation, etc.

Yet, important to note, though there may be a good number of "miraculous images" widely known and others unknown in out-of-the-way places, the author can produce very few *weeping* or *bleeding* sacred images from over the centuries. He can give you cures of the blind or even raisings from the dead by the dozen, whole books of prophecies, visions and private revelations, etc. He has simply not come across many weeping images where one might expect to find them. The author would welcome any reader pointing out any weeping image, from the past or present, not mentioned in this book.

But when it comes to the *20th* century, your author, as the reader will see, is aware of dozens of weeping and/or bleeding sacred images, two dozen such images in the last decade alone. More, both in Italy and in the United States there have been many weepings.

Most of the more famous weepings are connected with *Fatima* images or those honoring the *Immaculate Heart* of Mary. Perhaps there is a message there! For the Church! For the United States! For the World!

In the Eastern Church there have been a number of Marian apparitions and some weepings over the centuries. There was an apparition of Mary to Saint Romanos in 486 A.D. in which she told him not to despair because of his failure to improve his singing skills. Mary helped him to chant the hymns at the monastery in a sweet and melodious voice.

But there was weeping too as in 912 A.D. when the people of Constantinople were afflicted with a plague. They prayed for relief at the Church of Blachernae. First a certain Andres and an Epiphanius saw visions of Mary *weeping* and then an entire crowd did. After a short time Mary removed the veil from her head and held it over the assembly as a sign of protection. The feast known as the Protection of the Blessed Virgin is commemorated on October 1st.

During the night of April 13, 1185, a great fire destroyed the cathedral at Vladimir, Russia. Only the icon of Mary remained untouched. From then on the people prayed to the Mother of God before this icon when protection was needed; over the centuries they were saved from all kinds of tragedies.

In 1240 at the monastery of Pochaev the Mother of God (*Theotokos*) appeared as a fiery pillar, and a miraculous spring began filing with healing waters. Thousands of miracles have been recorded since. One of the greatest miracles of Pochaev was in 1675 when the monastery was being surrounded by the Tartars. A large group of monks saw the Virgin above the altar in a prayerful attitude and looking on them with loving kindness. The Tartar hordes retreated and the monastry was spared.

Other apparitions of Mary included appearances to the monk Saint Sergius and others in 1390, to the holy man Saint Aleksander in 1508, and to Saint Seraphim of Sarov of the Eastern Orthodox Church in 1830.

Concerning *tears* again, the icon at Mariapoch shed tears before large crowds in August, 1715, and in December, 1905. Many miracles occurred then.

Also at Klokochovo in the Uzh district of the Ukraine, an icon of Mary *shed tears* before a large crowd gathered for the Divine Liturgy. Similarly in Mikola, Rumania in 1699, a site of many cures.

It is significant that an International Fatima Pilgrim Virgin statue has been kept hidden in Moscow for some years.

Finally, as mentioned elsewhere, in 1968-9 there occurred the celebrated apparitions of Mary at the Coptic Church at Zeitun, Cairo, Egypt. Multitudes witnessed these, one of the most unusual series of Marian manifestations of all times, as was also the unusual and spectacular miracle of the sun spinning and descending at Fatima in our own times.

> "However, in certain places the Mother's presence is felt in a particularly vivid way." — Pope John Paul II at Fatima, May 13, 1982.

V — MARY HERSELF CRIES, TELLS OF HER TEARS

"Esther fell at his feet and tearfully implored him." **Est. 8:3.**

Before we look at modern and very recent tears of Mary and Jesus (vicariously shed through their various images) let us see some of the things *Mary,* in particular, has *said* about her *own* tears; or where *she shed* them personally in apparitions. We are not speaking here of weepings such as at Syracuse where an *image* shed tears.

We speak here either of Mary having been *seen* with tears or in tears in an apparition, or of she herself *mentioning* her tears. If we were also to include here Mary's speaking of her sufferings and sorrowings over the sad conditions in the world, we could expand this chapter enormously.

Let us go back a bit to the great "main-line" apparitions of Mary in modern times. At La Salette, France, Our Lady appeared, September 19, 1846, to the little shepherds Mélanie Mathieu-Calvat and Maximin Giraud. Mary was seated by a dry stream-bed, her head between her hands, and she was weeping — "her tears were flowing to the ground". Mary made prophecies then such as forecasting failures of crop harvests; the crops did fail and rot following her announcements. Other LaSalette prophecies of Mary still have meaning for our times.

At Pontmain, 1871, in a tableaux type apparition, Mary appeared ineffably sad as she clasped a blood-red crucifix.

Too few people realize that Our Lady also, reputedly, wept at Lourdes, Feb. 24, 1858. It was then that Bernadette turned to the crowd with serious face and urged repeatedly, "Penance! Penance! Penance!" *(pénitence).*

There is no claim, as far as I know, that Mary shed any tears at Fatima. Just before the great miracle of the spinning sun, however, October 13, 1917, Mary said that sinners should no longer offend Our Lord "Who is already too much offended." Mary was certainly not happy then. As the sun hurled downwards through the skies many of the 70,000 witnesses thought the end of the world and Judgment had come.

Berthe Petit (1870-1943), the Belgian mystic, a beautiful victim soul, travelled widely in Europe, though often ill, to propagate devotion to the Sorrowful and Immaculate Heart of Mary. This devotion is intimately and vitally tied-in with Fatima and Mary's other private revelations; and also with the safety of the world. Yes, even with the survival of much of the world in our own times.

We shall get to Mary's tears in a moment, in connection with Berthe, but there is a warmer and more significant liquid flowing from human bodies than tears. It is the flowing of blood.

On September 17, 1911, Mary appeared to Berthe in an apparition that demonstrated Mary's sympathetic compassion for the sufferings of her Son. It also stood as an encouragement to Berthe (as for anyone), who was required to suffer much as a victim soul.

Our Lady's brow was wounded and bleeding. Her hands and her heart were pierced as with the stigmata (In spirit and in heart — seven swords! — was not Mary the greatest "stigmatist" of all?). Mary told Berthe then: "You can now understand the sorrows which my Heart endured, the sufferings of my whole being for the salvation of the world."

Along these lines one might note that, on Good Friday, apparently March 29, 1918, Jesus appeared to Berthe. He was covered with blood.

To get to Mary's tears, in May, 1938, during one night of frightful suffering for Berthe, Mary consoled her with these words:

"All for my Son! Do not refuse human aid and comfort, your sufferings are beyond human endurance. But I am near you — the Mother who is watching over all your pains which are so pleasing to my Son. Give thanks to God Who has accepted your offerings, and taken it for the sanctification of your soul, for that of the clergy, and for the peace of the sad world."

Saying this, *two big tears* fell from the eyes of Our Lady. (It is good to recall later on, that sometimes, images of Mary seem to weep in sorrow over the sufferings of chosen souls.)

To Sister Elena Aiello (1895-1961) Mary also appeared in a terrible figure of suffering, and here too, we hear of Mary's tears. On Good Friday, April 16, 1954, Mary appeared to Sister Elena, in black. Seven swords were piercing her Immaculate Heart. She was sorrowful and *tears* were on her cheeks. Mary said then, "The wrath of God is near," and, "If men do not return to God with prayers and penance, the world will be overturned in a new and more terrible war."

On that same Good Friday, Jesus appeared to Sister Elena. He was covered with wounds and bleeding.

The following Good Friday, April 8, 1955, Mary appeared to Sister Elena and said, "Some nations will be purified, while others will disappear entirely." Mary said that while her *tears* fell. (We must note here that such prophecies, as those of Fatima, connected with the annihilation of several nations, are contingent for fulfillment on favorable, reparational human response or not.)

After Jesus appeared in 1959 to Sister Elena, "dripping with blood and with a painful and suffering look," and spoke of imminent ruin for the world, Elena says: "Then, the Madonna appeared to me, sad and shedding tears. She said: 'This great mantle which you see is the expression of my mercy for covering sinners and for saving them. Men, instead, cover themselves with even more filth, and do not want to confess their real faults. Therefore, the justice of God will pass over the sinful world to purify humanity for so many sins, openly committed and hidden, especially those which corrupt youth!' "

That we can bank on Sister Elena's authenticity — she was a stigmatist, too — as a genuine mystic and an instrument of heavenly messages, we have the miracle of the masonite panel near Sister Elena's bed. It bled with human blood and finally formed the face of Christ in agony. This began on September 29, 1955, feast of Saint Michael to whom Elena had fervently prayed for help and protection. Blood flowed from midnight, September 29 to October 13, 1955. The blood flowed many times, in 1955 and 1956 and intermittently to the death of Sister Elena (1961).

The blood was analyzed as human. The features of the face became clearer on feasts connected with the mysteries of the sufferings of the Redeemer and of His Blessed Mother. The blood flowed especially from the eyes and recalled to mind the image of Jesus in His Passion.

Prominent people, like a pontifical assistant, the mayor of the town, etc., were among the witnesses. We note here that Sister Elena was a very practical and balanced person, foundress and superioress (superior general) of the Minim Sisters. She arranged for the competent care of many orphans. She prophetically warned Mussolini about his wrong course of action which would lead to disaster. She was no unreliable person.

"Marguerite" is a pseudonym to protect the privacy of a modern Belgian mother. It is also the title of a truly amazing book that becomes more and more widespread and influential. It contains many wonderful and well-established communications of Our Lord to "Marguerite". (I do not give such praise idly; I recommend the book's trial reading for one's spiritual good. — see bibliography.)

For our purpose we make a very small extract where Marguerite tells of Mary (who also occasionally speaks) when seen by her in a crying episode. As Marguerite described the scene:

"On her gentle face there are tears and my heart is deeply stirred. To console her I hold out her Child to her, and He returns docilely to sit on the knees of His holy and august Mother. Her tears cease at once . . ." (Earlier, the Child had come from Mary to Marguerite's arms.)

Years later, in 1965, Marguerite comments: "I asked Our Lady the cause of her tears. Our Lady said:

" 'I wept over the horrors of the present world. I wept over the follies of the people who themselves forge the weapons of their destruction. I wept over the ingratitude of my children.' "

One simple observation: If Mary wept over such evils years ago, how much more has she to weep over today?

There is another mother, a Hungarian. We are not able to have as much information as we would like on the alleged private revelations communciatd to her, because she is in a Communist dominated country behind the Iron Curtain. Literature does increase about her. We report it, as some few other matters in this book, as simply news, if nothing else. This, as all marvels reported in this book, we leave to the final judgment of the Church. But we do say, *final* and *authoritative*.

About this Hungarian mother, *The Flame of the Immaculate Heart of Mary* is the title of a booklet translated from the Hungarian. It appeared earlier in the monthly magazine, *Das Zeichen Mariens,* Aug.-Sept. issues, 1976. Also under the title, *Die Libesflamme.* It claims a *Nihil Obstat* of the Diocesan Court of *Szekesfeherver,* Hungary, September 26, 1978. A message from this Hungarian mother from Mary, was sent by an authorized bishop to the Vatican.

In a brief statement Jesus once reportedly made to this Hungarian mother we hear Him say: "I am the Blood-donor of the world!"

Mary once said to the Hungarian mother: "You are a mother too. I share with you all the sorrow of my Heart. Imagine, if only one of your six children were to be damned! What sorrow it would mean to you! And yet, to my torment, I have to watch so many of my children go to damnation. Help! Help! Help me, my child!"

What a pitiful plea from Mary, the Mother of all! It prepares the way for our "tears" insertion. Between 1961 and 1974, Mary pleaded with the world continuously, tenderly and firmly through this Hungarian mother. On January 12, 1974, Mary told her sorrowfully:

"You implore me? I implore you! You are weeping? I am sobbing."

On a certain Friday the Blessed Mother had just finished saying: "My daughter, I extend to you my Heart's Flame of Love. Light your own heart with it and give it to at least one soul . . ." (Quoting the mother): "At this point the Virgin Mother began sobbing so hard that

"Little One, like my Son cried for Jerusalem, so do I cry for the City of Man. It is not too late to save your souls and draw close to Him Who died on the Cross for all mankind. — Great tribulations are at hand, but God's mercy is infinite."

Similar expressions of concern for "The City of Man" crop up in many modern prophetic utterances or private revelations.

Let me mention here another short appeal of Mary in an alleged apparition in France. It fits in well with the rest:

"I try to touch your hearts with my tears."

We believe that other such utterances concerning her tears or tearful appearances of Mary exist around the world and will become known and spread in due time, such as the reported apparition of Mary in Skiemonys, a village in the Diocese of Panevezys, Lithunaia, July 1962, under fierce Iron Curtain persecution. Mary appeared then to young Roma Pranciski working on a collective farm. Mary appeared *weeping* over Lithunia and asked for Friday fasting to bring atheists back to God.

To move southeast to Egypt, at Zeitoun, Cairo, 1968-1971, Our Lady did not weep nor did she speak at all, but she was sad at times. As Bishop Gregorius of the Coptic Church described one apparition atop the cathedral-like Coptic church in Zeitoun:

"She appeared larger than natural size, young, beautiful, all in light. It was the colour of the sky in Egypt. She wore something on her head like a veil. She looked down toward the cross on the main dome. She looked like the Sorrowful Mother. She did not look happy. She stood for as much as two or three hours in the same spot . . ."

Of another apparition there he said: "She looks somewhat happy and smiling, but somewhat sad, always kindly."

Marie-Julie Jahenny (1850-1941) stigmatist of Blain, France, is credited with many prophecies. Yves Dupont quotes her in *Catholic Prophecy*. The Church will rarely say anything about private prophecies. Only time will prove their fulfillment. And sometimes they are fulfilled when they seemingly are not because one half of the prophetic coin turns up, that is, because of the requested reparation a disaster, forecast otherwise, is averted. The prophecy has been fulfilled in the happier outcome of the double-sided forecast.

Concerning Marie-Julie Jahenny, we simply quote some lines where there is reference to "tears" as one might reportorially of facts or some news claimed, and from the book, *Prophecies of La Fraudais*. It is claimed that the famous Dr. Imbert-Gourbeyre, author of *La Stigmatisation et L'extase Divine,* put together texts from Marie-Julie's ecstasies that confirmed the La Salette prophecies. The doctor, though long deceased, still remains the most famous author on stigmatists.

As far back as November 29, 1877, the Blessed Mother reputedly said to Marie-Julie: "I prayed, I cried, I suffered . . . I came down on earth to warn them. I promised them salvation if they made penance . . . I have shed tears over France . . ."

"Shedding a few tears, the Blessed Virgin lets me see the incendiary flames arising above the Center (Paris) and the fire kindled in the midst of terrible battles . . ." "Only blackened walls were left of those temples upon which the Blessed Virgin had shed tears."

Of these flames on earth the Blessed Mother said with sighs:

"Daughter, men kindle it, and Satan blows upon it."

The last words are surely a true and graphic description of the cooperation of men and demons in evil works. The holy Père Lamy in the same France also gave a dramatic picture of the desolation to come some day on Paris. The above communications of Marie-Julie were of October 19, 1882.

"I still have in my eyes," the Blessed Mother told her, "the remains of the tears I shed on a similar day, while wishing to bring the good news to my children, if they would be converted, but the sad news if they were to persevere in their wickedness. Little attention has been paid to what I revealed . . ."

"Well then! I assure you that all these promises, my intimate secrets, are to be fulfilled. They must take place in a visible way . . . When I see what awaits the earth, my tears run down again." — September 29, 1901.

There are other references to Mary's tears and sorrows in the prophecies of La Fraudais, namely of Marie-Julie Jahenny, but have we not seen enough in this chapter!

(In his book, *The Last Times,* the well-known author, Rev. Benjamin Martin Sanchez, Doctor of Sacred Scripture, refers to Maria Julia Jahenny, and to her gift of prophecy "to a high degree". His book has the imprimatur.)

Despite our coverage of Mary's tears so far, it would seem very suitable to add here the story of the weeping of Our Lady of Siluva, Lithuania, because it has a good lesson for our days.

The little Baltic Sea country has endured much for the sake of the Catholic Faith over the centuries. With the advent of Protestanism the nobles became Lutherans in 1532, then Calvinists in 1551. The peasants remained loyal to Catholicism.

Though the Lithuanians had become Catholic in or around 1251, the little town of Siluva only built its first Catholic Church in 1457 under the title of the Nativity of Mary, the feast of Our Lady's birthday, September 8th. When the Calvinists came into power they began to appropriate everything Catholic and by 1570 the Catholics lost their church at Siluva. Before the last Catholic pastor departed he buried a favorite image of the Madonna and Child along with some vestments and important documents in a metal-covered oak chest. The burial site was about a half-mile from the church, near a huge rock. For some years things remained thus.

In 1588 new legislation favored Catholic rights. Catholics could repossess the properties unjustly taken from them; but they had to produce the documents necessary to prove ownership.

Twenty years later, one hot day in the summer of 1608, a number of children were playing around a huge rock in Siluva. They were astonished to see a beautiful lady with a child in her arms, standing on the rock. She was weeping. One child reported this to the Calvinist teacher. He claimed that it was the devil trying to draw Calvinists away from their new Protestant religion. But on the following day many people assembled at the rock of the apparition. Here the Calvinist teacher berated them for paying attention to the tales of mere children.

While he was still speaking all were frightened when the same weeping lady with the child in her arms again appeared. The Calvinist teacher managed to get control of himself and he asked the lady:

"Why are you weeping?"

"Formerly", she replied, "in this place my Son was adored and honored, but now all that the people do is seed and cultivate the land."

With that, the lady disappeared.

Despite opposition, an old blind man became the leader of the people who believed that the lady was the Blessed Virgin Mother with her Son held in her arms. The old man recalled the actions of the last pastor years ago. When led to the vicinity of the rock his blindness left him. He was then able to point out the place where to dig and the chest with the Marian image and important papers was unearthed. It took ten years of court battles before the tribunal at Vilnius, in 1622, decided in favor of the Catholics.

Successive churches were built over the years at Siluva and ever-larger chapels around the rock. The original buried image of the Madonna and Child (a replica of Saint Luke's Madonna and Child) was placed in the church at Siluva. The cult was approved by the local ordinaries and by Pope Pius VI in 1775.

Siluva remains the great Marian shrine of Lithuania oppressed and persecuted as the Lithuanian Catholics have been under the Communist government of the Russian Occupation since 1940. Pilgrims defy government regulations and harassment to visit Our Lady of Siluva and to pray for their persecuted country. Fortunate Americans can visit a beautiful chapel of Our Lady of Siluva in the National Shrine of the Immaculate Conception of Mary at Washington, D.C. and pray there for the liberation of their afflicted brethren.

The origins and history of this Marian Shrine of the Weeping Madonna at Siluva have great symbolism and significance for many Catholic or once Catholic areas in the world today. The Blessed Mother wept then because Her Son was no longer adored and honored where He once reigned.

She weeps today for similar reasons. Mary weeps because many places of Catholic adoration formerly flourishing have been wiped out or secularized by atheistic and Communist governments. Mary weeps because many Catholics, who enjoy freedom and religious liberty, neglect her Son in the Holy Eucharist, and leave their churches locked or empty of adorers of their Lord present in the Blessed Sacrament.

In the work, *The Queen of Heaven to Her Beloved Sons the Priests,* by Canon Paolo Viti, translated into English by Rev. Charles D. Gorman, with imprimatur of Cardinal O'Boyle, we have some messages of the Blessed Virgin Mother given through a chosen unnamed soul in Italy not long ago. There are a number of references to the sorrow and sadness of the Blessed Virgin Mother.

We give one:

"My sons, listen to me . . ." "I love you with a great love! Even though I find among you some who sadden my heart and cause me to shed bitter tears of sorrow."

Poor Blessed Mother! *Fac me tecum plangere!* Let me weep with you!

In the *Mystical City of God* revelations of the Venerable Mary of Agreda we have this description (vision) of the Blessed Mother receiving the dead crucified body of her Son in her arms:

> "This was to her an event of mixed sorrow and consolation; for in seeing Him thus wounded and all His Beauty disfigured

beyond all children of men, the sorrows of her most chaste Heart were again renewed; and holding Him in her arms and at her breast, her incomparable sorrow was rejoiced and her love satiated by the possession of her Treasure. She looked upon Him with supreme worship and reverence, shedding tears of blood."

Today we have *super-Pietas!*

Let us close here by bringing in a lady in America who is currently becoming better known. She is of Italian birth and resident in a mid-western city. It seems well established (in a national United States Catholic magazine) that she was granted a personal miraculous cure a few years ago. She apparently has the stigmata and wears gloves with the fingertips cut off. Considering her educational background, or lack of it, she speaks on religious subjects with unusual correctness and unction. She has a spiritual director and has been received well by persons familiar with mystics.

In apparitions of Mary she claims to have seen the Blessed Mother weep. Tears have been witnessed on her fair-sized American-made Fatima statue. This apparently genuine mystic claims a mission from Mary of: "Bring my children back to God."

"Surely we cannot help speaking of what we have heard and seen." Acts 5:20.

First Fatima statue of "CE" weeping, New Orleans, June 5, 1975

VI — MARY SPEAKS TO HER BELOVED PRIESTS, AND WEEPS

"The altar of the Lord you cover with tears." **Mal. 2:13.**

The "Marian Movement of Priests" (with lay associates in Cenacles of Prayer) is one of those quiet but powerful spiritual factors at work today to bring about a genuine renewal in the Church, and the eventual triumph of the Immaculate Heart of Mary over atheistic Communism and other evils.

We treat of the "Movement" briefly here, in a separate chapter, because of its uniqueness and importance, but again only from the viewpoint of considering Mary's tears about which we learn from the book of the movement, *Our Lady Speaks to Her Beloved Priests.*

This tear phenomenon, one can see, and see more plainly as we progress in our book, is a world-wide manifestation of Our Lady's feelings. If we hear of more manifestations of tears on the part of Mary, than of Christ, it does not mean that Christ has not made private manifestations of His own grief in recent years. He has imparted a number of such private revelations some of which have been connected *manifestedly* with several persons mentioned in this our book.

However, we can expect more tears from a *Mother* who sees many of her children suffering under great burdens, or living in sin in immediate danger of the eternal loss of their immortal souls. In these sad days Mary is accenting the fact that *She* is a *Mother*. Besides, it becomes more and more evident that God has given Mary a very special part and mission in the renewal of the Church, the overthrow of Communism, and the promised era of peace in the Church and world. Many, many movements, private revelations, utterances of seers, prophecies all go together and unify in a divine directive of common teaching content which also announces the eventual triumph of the Church.

Not long before the time when the North American International Fatima Pilgrim Virgin statue wept dramatically at New Orleans, Don Stefano Gobbi of the Milan archdiocese, received an inspiration for the Marian Movement of Priests when at Fatima on pilgrimage, May 1972. By July 1973 his spiritual director was confirming the first interior locutions from Mary to Father Gobbi as such; an initial small booklet was privately published.

This book has steadily increased in size with new locutions under the title, *Our Lady Speaks to Her Beloved Priests,* and has been published in soft-cover book form in an incredible number of editions in endless languages all over the world. Yet the book has no regular publishers, distributors, advertising or commercial sale. For instance, the English editions in the United States have numbered 10, 20, 30, 40, 50 thousand copies at a time and were undertaken on simple and pure faith. Significantly its frontpiece photo is of a strikingly beautiful Our Lady of Fatima statue in its upper part.

Our Lady Speaks to Her Beloved Priests is the official book of "The Marian Movement of Priests" and its associates. When Father Gobbi protested to Mary that he was not in the least equipped to head or direct the Movement, Mary agreed and declared it was *Her* Movement and *Her* Book and she would take care of everything. Those priest members, who are familiar with the Movement from the beginning, are all well aware that Mary has done just that. And the Movement, book and spirit continue to spread to remote corners of the world.

The wonder of the Movement and its book spreading so much and so far is that the book consists of private locutions and the clergy are usually the most cautious about receiving such. Yet the Movement, which is inspired by the words of Our Lady, has over 40,000 priest members around the whole world and includes a good number of cardinals and bishops. Pope John Paul II has received Father Gobbi privately and honored him by letting him concelebrate Mass with himself, the Pope, in his private chapel. We mention these things to give additional value to what we refer to in the book, *Our Lady Speaks to Her Beloved Priests,* again only what is *ad rem* or pertinent to our main subject.

First, concerning one of the numerous Marian images that have wept in Italy in recent years, Mary, on July 13, 1973, thanked Father Gobbi for offering Mass before that image of her:

"How I appreciated the homage you rendered me this morning! You came to Ravenna to celebrate Mass before my image that sheds tears, wishing to console my Immaculate Heart. How I rejoiced at your intention: so filial, so affectionate, and so delicate!

"Yes, you truly consoled me; you changed my tears into smiles, my sorrows into joy.

"I smiled and blessed you."

Mary went on to explain the reason for her tears, that they were the tears of a Mother weeping over her children. It was because many of them were forgetful of God, steeped in sins of the flesh and heading for irreparable ruin. She said that many of her tears would be wasted on a large number of sinners because of their indifference.

What hurt Mary most, she said, was that some of her priest sons, her chosen and consecrated ones, contributed most to her tears because of their lack of love for her, their not listening to her Son's promises, their neglect of Him in the Blessed Sacrament and their abandonment of Him in the tabernacle. She welcomed the Marian Movement of Priests and blessed it.

Among 1972 Marian weepings, human tears were reported as coming from a Fatima image at Ravenna and with one photo showing a tear suspended from the chin, December 9, 1972. We might note here, too, that in the year previous to the above declarations of Mary about her tears, there were many famous weepings of Fatima statues in the United States.

On December 1, 1973, Mary spoke to Father Gobbi about the great evil of atheism and of some unbelieving priests, who wore the guise of lambs but who were real wolves within the Church. She spoke of God's justice which would soon break loose against Satan and his camp because of the love, prayers and sufferings of the elect. If men only knew, Mary said, of the great and inexpressible tribulations in the making, they might be converted.

Then Mary complained: "But who has listened to my messages, who has understood the meaning of my tears, of my maternal invitations?" It was due to the few rare and ignored souls who did pay attention that the chastisement had been pushed back. It might be commented here that we learn from various apparitions and private revelations, that the "threatened chastisement" has been pushed back again and again because of the reparation made by chosen souls and because of the intervention of Mary.

On December 19, 1973, Mary again acknowledged a visit of Father Gobbi and the offering of his Mass before the image of the Virgin of Tears.

On October 30, 1975, Mary spoke about the gatherings of priests (cenacles) consecrated to her Immaculate Heart and of their need for consolation and encouragement. She said that the time had come when she would make herself more evident in the Church which she called "my Church", by ever more striking signs. (We must recall that Mary has the title, "Mother of the Church", given to her at Vatican II.)

"My tears are shed in many places to bring them all back (errant priests) to my sorrowful Heart of a Mother.

"The tears of a Mother succeed in moving even the most hardened hearts. Now, even my tears of blood leave so many of my sons completely indifferent!

"My messages will multiply all the more when the voices of my ministers refuse to proclaim the Truth."

Mary went on to point out important truths that were neglected in preaching: heaven, the Cross that saves, sin that wounds Her Heart and that of Jesus; hell; the need for prayer and penance.

Mary mentioned that her tears were shed in many places. It was in June, 1975, that the first Fatima statue of the Cuban exile, "CE" began a series of weepings. There were other weepings in Italy. Mary's reference to her tears of *blood* probably called attention to Marian images that shed blood, such as at Porto San Stefano in 1972, and at Maropati. Also at Madrid, where one title of the weeping Marian image there was that of "Mother of Priests."

These blood tears were to increase shortly, in March, April and May, 1976, on the image of the Sorrowful and Immaculate Heart of Mary, of the stigmatist, Teresa Musco, lay woman of Caserta, not far from Rome. (Incidentally Father Gobbi visited Teresa, and, as I understand from a good source, reported to a bishop on one of the weepings.)

The comment might be made here that it is obvious to anyone cognizant of certain conditions and happenings in the Church, that there is much cause for the tears of Mary, either personal, spoken of by her, or vicariously shed through her many images, even tears of blood. When, we might ask, in all the history of the Church have appeared so many serious, sorrowful and striking signs- — "Signs of the Times!"

It is important to remember also what Mary said above about her *messages* multiplying. We can see that many things hang together from around the world. Putting them together would be very helpful for all, but especially for the enlightenment of bishops and priests.

On January 21, 1978, Mary expressed to Father Gobbi such anguish on her part as never before experienced. She was pleading, begging for help from her priest sons on all sides and backing up her pleas with reference to various unusual supernatural manifestations: "I am pleading with you through manifestations that are becoming more numerous and more evident: my tears, my apparitions, my messages."

Mary was begging help from her priest sons to prevent a terrible war of incredible violence with countless victims and blood flowing on all sides.

We might comment here again on the urgency of Mary's pleas and tears; and how the multitude of evils in the world document her words, as also the manifold unusual signs back up her messages. Priests in particular should listen to these salvos of claims as to the authenticity of Mary's mission in the modern world. Further, they have a terrible responsibility where they ignore such numerous obvious signs, and where they do not take the time and means to protect seers and to foster the cause of genuine messengers of Mary who present authentic signs given to endorse them. One cannot note carelessly nor ignore God's manifest dispensation of signs, gifts and graces. Such attitudes can have implications of unintended blasphemy.

Note — to return to our main subject — that since Mary's 1978 declaration above as to her tears becoming more evident, the exile gentleman from Cuba ("CE") received a second Fatima statue that wept about a dozen times in June 1980. The lady exile from Poland, "AW", found her own Fatima statue weeping again at the times of the assassination attempts on President Regan and Pope John Paul II. Other Fatima statues in Louisiana have had limited weepings. There have been claims of other Fatima statues weeping elsewhere.

It is well to note again that weeping Marian images are often *Fatima* statues. Such selective miraculous weepings can only suggest certain obvious connections *with Fatima* and the entire *Fatima message.* Besides such weeping Fatima images of great fame, we can only guess how many of Mary's images, including other Fatima ones, have wept throughout the world in recent years; as an exhaustive survey might reveal.

Finally, with reference to Mary and Father Gobbi, on Good Friday, April 13, 1979, Mary sounded hope in the resurrection of the Church after the sufferings of purification. Mary said that she lived beneath the Cross, because, as a Mother, she must help her Son to die and that her place was to be near Him when He died.

"And now my sorrow bursts forth like a flooding river that bursts through all its dikes. My tears bathe His countenance, my laments cradle His body, and with my hands I close the deep wounds while my Immaculate Heart becomes His first sepulcher."

Mary added that her prayer would pierce the heavens and be heard by the Father. He would shorten her anguished waiting and for her sake *anticipate* the moment of her Son's Resurrection. All this has deep, mystical and real meaning for the Church in the world of today — and especially for Mary's priest sons.

I suggest an open-minded reading of the book, *Our Lady Speaks to Her Beloved Priests*, to all who have not read it. It has hundreds of pages of solid doctrine and Marian spirituality for our times. It is intended for lay associates also. Not as yet in the book at this writing, Our Lady said on July 1, 1981 that the struggle between Herself as "the Woman clothed with the Sun", and the Red Dragon, had entered into its conclusive phase.

She asked, that in the Spirit of Wisdom one realize how to read the *Signs of the Times* in which we are now living.

On that same July 1, 1981, Mary gave the "first" of her beloved sons, Pope John Paul II, "bathed in his own blood", as an example to follow in great suffering.

It may well be that many have missed the greatest of all other signs given in our day: Our Holy Father, Pope John Paul II.

An after thought! It has been reported to this author that Father Gobbi himself not long ago witnessed an image of Our Lady of the Nations (such an image might also be called, "Our Lady of All Peoples") weeping in Japan. This seems to be a modern, plain, flowing-lines statue carved from wood with a cross behind the back of Mary and she standing on a globe. The author has been informed by a well-known priest that a Japanese bishop saw the statue weep many times. The location of the statue was given as Akita, Japan.

(At this writing a new, seventh edition of *Our Lady Speaks to Her Beloved Priests* is forthcoming.)

"I love you with a great love! Even though I find among you some who sadden my Heart and cause me to shed bitter tears of sorrow." — Mary in *The Queen of Heaven to Her Beloved Sons,* Canon Paolo Viti.

Tearful-looking North American Pilgrim Virgin, summer, 1972

VII — SYRACUSE — BIG "SPLASH" OF TEARS IN OUR TIMES

"Do not the tears stream down her cheek?" **Sir. 35:15.**

During early Saturday morning, August 29, 1953, young Antonietta Jannuso, recently married, was suffering from an unusual malady which had attacked her after her pregnancy. She lay in bed with violent convulsions. At 8:30 a.m. she was plunged into darkness. Normally spasms would strike her then but this time none came; her eyes opened clearly and fell on the image of the little Madonna, the *Madonnina* on the wall.

Unbelieving at first, stunned, Antonietta saw two tears, one in either eye of the image of the Immaculate Heart of Mary which was made of pure plaster. The image of Mary stood out in relief from its glass backing. Mary's right hand was placed gracefully in large part over her Heart, which was painted red with a flame mounting from it, rosettes around it, and sets of triple rays spreading from it.

Antonietta screamed, "The Madonna — Look, the Madonna is weeping!"

Beside her bed were her sister-in-law Grazia, and the older Concerta Sgarlata who thought Antonietta delirious. But they too looked and now there was a constant stream or flow of tears from both eyes of the little Madonna. Mary's eyes brightened and she seemed human, as a living woman who weeps. With the resounding cries of the women, neighbors began to run into the humble Jannuso home (actually that of Antonietta's husband's brother Giuseppe).

"There is a virgin crying! — at the *via degli Orti.*"

The stream of Mary's tears continued with some interludes for *four* days. The initial stream of the first thrilled spectators swelled to actual millions; and this in a city, Syracuse, Sicily, of only 80,000 inhabitants. They flowed in from Sicily and also the Italian mainland. Unbelievers fell on their knees; lax Catholics or "Communist" Catholics were changed: confessions quadrupled.

The Police, hard-put to maintain order, commandeered the statue. A peace officer carrying the statue to Police Headquarters of *Via Roma* had his uniform vest soaked with the continually flowing, warm tears.

After the officers removed all removable parts of the image and made a thorough inspection, their conclusion was that the tears emanated from the eyes only. The statue reconstituted, they fell on their knees. Then Angelo Jannuso happily carried it back home but only with a long struggle through dense crowds.

The *"Lacrimazione"* or weeping of tears, continued for the four days of August 29, Sunday Aug. 30, Aug. 31, and September 1st. On the final day of weeping a scientific commission secured some of the last tear liquid. Laboratory analysis showed the same chemical content as human tears have.

Many persons had touched cloths (or even "soaked" them) in the running or falling tear liquid. In the meantime the sick and infirm of all types were converging from all Italy on the *via degli Orti* or street of the Jannuso home. Significantly this area had been designated as *"Strada dell' inferno"* or "Hell Row", because of various adverse conditions. Now, as to the original garbage dump area of Lourdes, the trusting and hopeful faithful came. It was like Gospel scenes again of faith, love—and healing.

In the first few days after the weepings, cures, with or without use of tear-touched cloths, began to abound, in Syracuse, over Sicily and beyond, to Italy and the far places of the world.

It is not our purpose here to establish the miracles and cures, the spiritual conversions and favors that have been claimed, credibly so, through the intercession of Our Lady of Syracuse; they were in great numbers, worked even by the hundreds in the very first year. Secular and even liberal journals recounted their numbers day by day.

We suggest a very good book that captures the whole scene and atmosphere of the early days of the weeping Madonna of Syracuse. It is *Look—the Madonna is Weeping,* by H. Jongen, S.M.M. of the De Montfort Fathers.

After many investigations the Bishops of Sicily at their regular conference, December 10 and 11, 1953, unanimously concurred that there could be no doubt as to the reality of the tears. Rome stated, through the *Osservatore Romano,* December 18, 1953: "They (the Bishops) have expressed the sincere desire that this manifestation of our heavenly Mother may inspire the whole world with a true spirit of penance, and more fervent devotion to the Immaculate Heart of Mary. It is likewise their wish that a spiritual edifice be erected to commemorate the miracle."

Since then Syracuse of Our Lady of Tears has become a frequented shrine with a great church edifice, accommodations, facilities, etc., for streams of pilgrims from all over the world.

Why Syracuse? Why this great explosion of tears so unique in history? While there were other claimed weepings in Italy before that at Syracuse, and many after 1953, no Italian site, as far as I can determine, has become such a great international place of pilgrimage as Our Lady of Tears, the place of the Weeping Madonna of Syracuse.

One might make a few observations. Sicily has had a long, tortured history of invasions, wars and much suffering. Sicily has been a land of much poverty (the Jannusos were of the poor laboring or working class). Sicily has much illiteracy. Sicily at the time of the weepings had much Communistic infiltration and laxity among "Catholics". And, as Pope John Paul II enunciated clearly recently the land is plagued with the Mafia operations.

But Sicily also has had many shrines and sanctuaries to Mary with famous ones at Palermo and Viceri. Pius XII called Sicily, "Mary's fief". He also spoke to the Sicilian People of "the enemies of Religion in your Island."

Sicily needed protection, Sicily needed encouragement, Sicily needed change. Is Sicily not a symbol for the world? Do not the tears of Mary cry to the world!

At Syracuse Mary "wept" in a lowly home, in a lowly neighborhood, in the room of a Communist-sympathizing husband. Why Sicily, and not Italy for such a great lacrimation and great miraculous shrine? Italy would soon get many further individual and isolated weepings as we shall see. Has Sicily, a lowly province compared to mainland Italy, some special part to play or thing to do, a heritage to preserve in coming years?

In Sicily some years ago, where there have been some special "seers", little children, one was given a visual cartoon, like a pictured prophecy, concerning Italy. In it Italy is depicted as running with several rivers of blood which transverse it. This author is familiar with other "prophecies" from this source and with some evident fulfillment of them in recent years. It is merely conjectural, but there could be a vital connection between Sicily's Madonna of the Tears and Italy's future.

A final observation: the image through which Mary chose to express her maternal weeping was that of the Immaculate Heart of Mary. She could have chosen any one of numerous other Marian images by various titles. But by choosing that of her Immaculate Heart Mary makes a direct reference to her Fatima apparitions and prophecies. Also to Berthe Petit's mission — because of Mary's image and tears — of spreading devotion to the *Sorrowful and Immaculate Heart of Mary*. A Sorrowful Heart of Mary is surely one connected with tears!

Is it strange then, that, emanating from Fatima, Portugal and Milano, Italy, Father Gobbi's "Marian Movement of Priests" has, as a prime requirement, consecration to the Immaculate Heart of Mary?

It seems that many, many things are hanging together, supernaturally, in our twentieth century, the century of Our Blessed Mother's tears.

Recall also, that Our Lord told Berthe Petit, that the devotion to the Sorrowful and Immaculate Heart of Mary was the last of the helps He would give to save the world.

Nor is it simply an idle thought to predict, that these tears of Mary at the foot of the Cross, relayed as it were through her many images, especially in a great outpouring as at Syracuse, to our own "time zone", are part of a co-redemptive action on her part that will eventually and definitively lead to the establishment of the titles, "Co-Redemptrix" and "Mediatrix of All Graces" for Mary. That we leave to the Church. But we can privately pray for it. (In May 1983 Mount Aetna was spewing forth a red lava stream in Sicily. Other volcanoes elsewhere have also been active. Twenty-two eruptions, worldwide within a year!)

> "When one part of the atmosphere moves, another part feels the kick." — Eugene Rasmusson, National Oceanic and Atmospheric Administration. (1983)

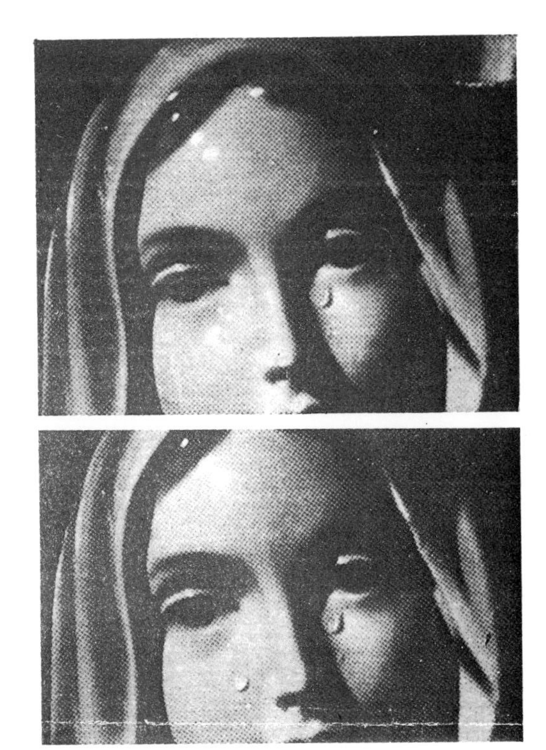

Weeping Immaculate Heart of Mary image, Syracuse, Aug. 29, 1953

VIII — WEEPING MARIAN IMAGES OUTSIDE ITALY AND UNITED STATES

"Before God my eyes drop tears." **Jb. 16:20.**

To be honest this author is not acquainted with a good number of weeping statues in other single nations than Italy and the United States— and that is part of the burden, and surely the message of this book. The two greatest powers in the world, the Catholic Church in Rome and Italy, in the spiritual order, and the United States in the political, have been favored, or warned, and probably, more correctly, both, with a large number of weeping images.

It also happens that atheistic Communism (mainly empowered in Russia) is the sworn arch-enemy of both the United States and the Catholic Church. As Russia and widespread Communism have made many religious and political martyrs in this century already, many more of both type martyrs are in the planning, in the offing.

This helps us to understand, why, in Father Gobbi's book, Mary declares she is the Woman Clothed with the Sun and her great battle is on with the Red Dragon. The Dragon personifies Satan in the atheistic challenge to oust God from His heavens and His earth. Lucifer, in the beginning wanted to get rid of God, and his arch-instrument today, expressing his satanic nature so utterly, is atheism and predominantly atheistic Communism.

And it is not without note that beside being "Red", the representation of all this evil in the Twelfth Chapter of *Revelation (Apocalypse)* is a "Dragon", and the dragon symbol is typical of atheistic China, the other immense, rising Communist power.

This author, however, is convinced, and, in part from rumors and brief reports he hears at times, that time and research would bring to light other weeping statues the world around, now unheard of by many, especially by Americans. But he will tell of some.

In India, where there is so much devotion to Mary, there are famous Marian shrines as to Our Lady of Good Health at Vailan Kanni, Tanjore, T. Nadu; and many cures. Also at Bandra in Bombay, in honor of Our Lady of Prompt Succor. (Small world, as I write not far from the national — and original — U.S. shrine to Our Lady of Prompt Succor in New Orleans with its own miraculous image.) Also in the Cathedral of Saint Francis of Assisi at Ernakulam there is a Marian shrine.

To our main theme, however, for about ten years there has been a weeping statue of Mary at Poondy in T. Nadu, India.

It is very hard to establish anything happening behind the Iron Curtain, especially in remote areas of that vast sprawling territorial giant and with all sorts of persecution against, and restraints on Religion; and suppression of communication. But I am utterly convinced many marvelous things have happened to cheer and sustain those suffering multitudes. In *Explosion of the Supernatural,* concerning weeping images we hear: "there are dozens of cases behind the Iron Curtain and in the West."

We have mentioned the report of the Blessed Mother, at the village of Skiemonys *weeping* over Lithuania. I cannot say whether there was any weeping *image* involved. Lithuania has been under fearful persecution for years. The mere secret (only way) circulation of religious literature has sent young Lithuanian girls to the concentration camps or salt mines of Siberia. I have seen a copy of a prayerbook put together by such sufferers. Unusually touching!

In the U.S.S.R. other reported Marian apparition sites include Rostov, Kharkhov, Leningrad, etc. At Tombow, twenty-five miles south of Moscow, a white hand wrote in the sky for a half-hour. The writing or message was readable for three hours. If we cannot report factual tears in connection with the above alleged apparitions we can be certain the apparitions or messages had tearful and sorrowful elements.

If we diagonal from Lithuania to a southern ruled area of the U.S.S.R. to the Catholic Ukraine (Kruschev was known as "The Butcher of the Ukraine") twenty apparitions of Mary at Seredne were claimed from December 20, 1954 through November 21, 1955. The reported message was like that of Fatima, urgent warnings, penance, and a danger to Rome and the Holy Father mentioned (it seems that at least one interpretation was that it meant a spiritual danger or crisis).

This report came from *The Light,* a Ukranian monthly of the Basilian Fathers at Toronto. Again, no words about any weeping image, as so often has accompanied such twentieth century apparitions. Information is distressingly meager.

To move far northwards, some years ago, in what was a war-zone between Russia and East Prussia, at Girkalnis (Lat. 55:19N, Long. 23.13E) several apparitions of Mary were reported. In a village church Mary settled in a cloud above the Tabernacle. All present in the church saw Her. In the cloud were brilliant stars (believed to be symbols for saints). Mary spoke but little:

"I am the Mother of Mercy and wish to be known by that name."

"How long will you remain with us?"

"I will remain with you to the end."

As Emmett Culligan states, this report came through the Marian Hill Fathers of Detroit. (*The Last World War and the End of Time,* p. 180)

In these two latter Iron Curtain reports there is no mention of tears, but I have included them, as in a few other cases, because full information is so lacking, and they, I am sure, are but a few examples of Mary's activity behind the Iron Curtain and her tears. (We have seen the Hungarian mother.) And interestingly enough, the "Mother of Mercy" title reminds us that in neighboring Soviet dominated Poland, Our Lord gave His "Mercy of God" revelations to Sister Faustina, which devotion was recently made acceptable since the ascendancy of Pope John Paul II who knew of Sister Faustina at close point. It all hangs together!

We must point out here that we could mention any number of Church-accepted and also new unpassed-on apparitions of Christ and Mary in our times, but we are mainly accenting happenings which involved "concrete" tears or references to them. So we have mentioned Our Lady *weeping* at La Salette.

We have not mentioned in detail Pellevoisin, Knock, Banneux, Beauraing to indicate a number of fairly recent European and approved Marian shrines. But they — and others unmentioned — are all important manifestations of the activity of Mary in our times. Only God knows in how many places around the world Mary has been active and still is! In his *Explosion* book Haffert speaks of some twenty reported and current apparitions.

Father Paul of Moll was a holy Benedictine priest with many wonders in his life. He had a friend in Ghent who had secured a *Pieta* of polychrome about 13 inches high. Father Paul blessed the *Pieta,* and, as he himself has testified, tears then flowed in abundance from both eyes of the Virgin. This was in 1893. This weeping was repeated very often in the presence of witnesses, one occasion being Thursday, September 20, 1894 for the space of two hours. This flow of tears occurred in the presence of Father Paul who gathered two or three of the tears in a little glass tube for one of the witnesses.

In the life of the holy French priest, Père Lamy, we read of a reference to the weeping image of Mary at La Pailly, "She is crying!" One afternoon, in the garden of Père Lamy at La Pailly, friends were with him and were gathering salad for dinner. It was a warm but lovely autumn day. One friend, Francis, looked at the statue of Mary and exclaimed: "The statue seems to be crying. Oh, look, Father!" Father Lamy came to look at it.

"Ah, yes," he said sadly, "She is crying. She may well suffer and feel pain, our dear Mother! Let us try to comfort Her." Father Lamy cut some roses on the right of the pathway, and had John-Peter run to the house for a chair.

"Get up on the chair, John-Peter, and dry the tears of our Dear Mother."

Père Lamy handed John-Peter the roses which the latter turned round and round in and over the tears which flowed from both eyes and down her breast like a stream as far as the girdle. John-Peter held the roses on the breast of the statue while they said a decade of the Rosary with Father Lamy, then responded to the Litany led by Father. Finally Father and John-Peter sang the *Salve Regina* together. This episode lasted about ten minutes, but the statue continued to weep much longer.

"The Blessed Virgin is sad. She weeps for our sins and our misfortunes." The actual year of this happening is not given, but the weeping seems to have occurred in the latter years of Père Lamy's life. Père talked with the Blessed Mother and the angels. He died in 1931.

If we move over to the near East a few years ago, 1977, the National Our Lady of Fatima Pilgrim Virgin statue of Syria wept and continued to weep. The statue wept in Damascus. I am not aware of the date of its last weeping. This news has come from a number of sources but the Blue Army has documentary evidence from the Bishop of Damascus. This author has pictures of this statue with tears, from Msgr. Dr. Georges Hafouri, pastor of the church at Koussour, Damas (Syria).

On Wednesday, July 20, 1977, after a morning Mass, one of those attending, Mme. Georgette Sofia saw the statue weeping.

"Come see, come see, the Virgin cries!" It was about 9:15 a.m. Others in the Church saw the statue's eyes filling up and the tears beginning to flow.

Again, significantly, this is a *national* and a *Fatima* Pilgrim Virgin statue, bearing the message of Fatima and weeping in Our Lady of Fatima Church in Damascus, where for some time we have, between Syria, Lebanon and Israel, a potentially worldwide explosive area. As with many miracles worked in recent years for persons of those areas, nationalities and faiths, miracles worked by intercession of the holy Lebanese Maronite hermit, Saint Sharbel, it seems despairingly late for people to benefit by great graces. Similarly they do not seem to have benefited much by the well-established apparitions of Mary at the Coptic church in Cairo (Zeitoun) to multitudes of Christians, Moslems and whomsoever; and with many miracles. Are great graces for unity and peace simply neglected? Or largely ignored?

The Chalice — and justice — runneth over!

The above Syrian Fatima Pilgrim Virgin statue weeping in such a recently (and still) troubled and war-risk area, in the judgment of this author, is one of the more significant of recent Fatima statue weepings! Mary weeps over her warring Christian Arabs and her Jewish and Moslem children! A great number of them, as she, are descendents of their common father, Abraham. (Since this original writing time we have experienced Israel's invasion of Lebanon!)

The magazine of the same Blue Army, *Soul* reported sometime ago a story from *Le Matin*, May 28th, in Haiti, that told of the alleged weeping of the Fatima statue that had been traveling in that country. It took place in the chapel attached to the cathedral. This does not seem to have been an extensive weeping and I am unaware if any final decision was made by the Archbishop of Port-au-Prince.

From a letter of Mr. Siko Laurent, Director of the Blue Army in Haiti, under date of le 7 février 1982, at Port-au-Prince, we have this information:

"Un matin, le mercredi 26 mai 1976, il y avait une grande agitation dans la ville: tout le monde disait avec inquietude: *'LA VIERGE PLEURE AU BICENTENAIRE, A LA CHAPELLE SIXTINE:'* Et beaucoup de personnes se pressaient pour aller voir le phénomène. La chapelle et les alentours étaient bondés de gens de tous milieux. Lá Télevision haitienne était sur les lieux pour filmer la statue. 'Télé-Haiti' possède donc ce fameux document."

In brief there was great excitement when word was rapidly spread that the statue of the Virgin in the Sistine Chapel was weeping and people of all classes poured into the chapel and the neighborhood. Television Haiti filmed the statue in a famous document.

The letter also tells how a tear rolled down the face to the chin, enlarged there and fell to the ground. It tells how a new tear took the same path and was at the middle of the cheek when photographed. The brilliance of the eyes and other factors were recounted such as the sadness expressed in the face. An account of a witness, Marie-Flore Thelus, can be found in the journal, *Le Nouvelliste* of May 29 and 30, 1976 (Haiti).

Whatever, the outcome of the Haiti claims, and though we wish to deny neither Mary or Jesus any rightful venerations to miraculous images, it matters little to our purpose here. There are so many well reported weepings in the world. But we want to get to some seemingly very significant and important weepings in Italy, and then those in our own United States, weepings unknown to a great number of Americans — and surely to their great loss; and danger.

Take, for a good instance, the weeping of the Mary statue in Madrid. We quote from Haffert's *Explosion of the Supernatural,* "In 1972 a statue of the Blessed Virgin in Madrid known as 'Queen of Victim Souls and Mother of Priests' bled from the eyes and heart eleven times."

This bloody weeping of so significantly a double-titled Marian image links dramatically such pleas as those of Mary in Father Gobbi's book *Our Lady Speaks To Her Beloved Priests,* and the vital reparational sufferings of victim souls and stigmatists, especially their sufferings for priests.

From Spain one can go over to far China. *Soul* magazine, September-October 1981, reports that the *Wall Street Journal* recently said: "A mysterious light appeared last year in a hilly, wooded area on the outskirts of Shanghai. For reasons difficult to fathom, word spread that the Virgin Mary had made an appearance."

Soul says that the light shone for three days over the very church of Our Lady of Zose on the hill outside Shanghai where a statue of the Immaculate Heart of Mary, in the very same church, is said to have wept tears for three days in 1953. Pilgrims hungry for God, Mary and the supernatural, have flocked to the church from all over China. (We have mentioned the Lady of All Nations' statue weeping in Japan.)

The Blue Army *Soul* magazine of March-April 1979, reporting on the alleged Vietnam apparitions of Our Lady of Fatima at Binh-Trieu Fatima Center, tells of Ho-Ngoc-Anh and his extraordinary experiences and cure. He is said to have received messages from Mary.

When the Blue Army took the Pilgrim Virgin statue through Vietnam in February, 1974, Ho-Ngoc-Anh thought he saw the statue weeping when it passed near him on its visit to the Cong-Hoa Military General Hospital. That same night about 4 a.m. Ho-Ngoc-Anh saw Our Lady standing in front of him. He was cured the next year on December 27th, a cure the local ecclesiastical authorities agreed was miraculous.

The author feels he must comment briefly on the recently reported Marian apparitions in Communist-held Yugoslavia to four girls and two boys in the Croatian area of Medjugorje. Allegedly the Blessed Mother first appeared on June 24, 1981 in the village of Medjugorje on the hill called Podbrdo. She was in gray and holding the Child Jesus in her arms. She told the children not to be afraid and to keep coming as she had "important things" to tell them. Mary identified herself as the "Queen of Peace" and asked for such a feast, and for fasting on bread and water to obtain peace in the world. She said the "world is on the edge of catastrophe."

Contrary to expectations, Mary appeared very sad on the feast of the Immaculate Conception, Dec. 8, 1981, knelt and prayed: "My Beloved

Son, forgive the world for so many sins!" A heart-rending plea of the Immaculate Mother of God!

There were at least ten visits of Mary reported as of November 1981. The eldest girl and boy asserted that the secrets entrusted to them did not frighten them but that their contents are both sad and happy. Mary requested prayer, penance and frequent reception of the Sacraments. Cures of a paralyzed boy, a blind man and a cancerous woman lend credulity to the genuineness of the apparitions which the local bishops seem to favor. The Yugoslavian Cardinal in Rome, Franjo Seper was quoted as saying there was no natural explanation of the events.

Although Mary appeared with a blue cape and a halo of small stars around her head her gown was gray. It will be interesting to follow these events and learn the full messages. Our Lady could only be sad over the conditions in Communist Yugoslavia. The local Communists reacted with hostility and have already sentenced the pastor, Rev. Jozo Zovko to three and a half years in prison. This reminds us of their recent alleged firing of a gun or cannon at the reported apparition of Mary at Havana. They fear Mary even as the Chinese Communists sought to destroy that Lady who was the head of the Legion of Mary. Their desperation is somewhat that of the devil who knows his hour of defeat by Mary is near.

We might almost close this chapter with a sort of "tears in reverse" of Mary. It has its message! When "Ancilla Domini", Magdalen of the Cross (d. 1919) (as a member of the Confraternity of Mary, Queen of Hearts) was a child of four, Mechtilde Schw-- living in the St. Louis parish of Munich, she felt very sympathetic toward Our Lady of Sorrows whose picture hung in her home.

When her mother would be gone Mechtilde would climb onto a chair before the picture. With her handkercief she would then endeavor to wipe away the tears of Mary. Miraculously the tears would disappear, and later miraculously reappear. Once when a blind beggar child had come, Mechtilde asked Our Lord, for the sake of those tears of His Mother, to give the blind child light. Mechtilde touched the child's eyes with her handkerchief and the child saw.

We pass over other wonders in Mechtilde's life, such as an animated crucifix, which, in the first year of her married life in Regensburg, spoke, saying to her: "My dearest daughter!" Or bilocation and the stigmata. And a great familiarity with the angels, including archangels like Michael and Gabriel. One might observe, cannot devotion to Our Lady's tears and heeding her requests wipe them away? Cannot Our Lady's, a Mother's tears make even the blind see!

It is a well established tradition that the Blessed Mother dwelt at the ancient city of Ephesus. It is the city of the ruins of the great basilica of

Saint Mary where the Council of Ephesus in 431 A.D. defined as dogma that Mary was truly entitled to be called *Theotokos* or Mother of God. A notable shrine there is Panaya Kapulu, the house reputedly where Our Lady dwelt, and visited by Pope Paul VI. Of three apparitions of Mary there since this century we present one briefly.

On August 13, 1902, Mary appeared to Helen, the daughter of the early caretaker, Andrea. Mary was in black, her arms crossed on her breast. It was outside the chapel toward which Mary turned her eyes while remaining still for about a half-hour. Her head remained bowed in an attitude of profound sadness. It was covered with a long veil which reached to either foot. At the end Mary rose with a white cloud that enveloped her to her knees, enclosed her at the crest of the hill, and with her disappeared there. Since then, in our days, there are many pilgrimages to Ephesus and Mary's house.

One might say Mary weeps because many of her children are not "at home" with her.

Ephesus also reminds us of St. John the Evangelist who had care of Mary there. The ruins of John's great basilica at Ephesus, like those of St. Mary's Basilica, are being restored by the Quatman family of Ohio. These modern discoveries and pilgrimages to Ephesus also remind us that not far away at Patmos John wrote the *Apocalypse* and about the "Woman Clothed with the Sun" confronting the Dragon.

To return to China for a moment, *Soul* magazine of July-August, 1982 says that Father Peter Hsiang, C.S.J.B., Director of the Chinese Catholic Apostolate, reports that "Our Lady appeared in China in 1978, in this apparition in Chiang Si province."

"Israel warns Syria not to play with fire." "Syria warns U.S. Marine blood could flow." — news reports, May 1983.

Padre Pio, stigmatist

IX — THE MOTHER OF THE CHURCH WEEPS IN THE LAND OF THE CHURCH

***"Coming within sight of the city, He wept over it . . ."* Lk. 19:41.**

Syracuse alone, nearly 30 years ago, should have been a grace large enough to turn Italy around, but Italy is no longer a truly Catholic nation. It is infested with Communism, laxity exists in church attendance, and there is much immorality. Witness recently, despite the pleas of Pope Paul II, with the Pope shot and on a bed of pain, a so-called "Catholic" country kept its pro-abortion laws on the books.

Hearts continue to harden. Hundreds of thousands may acclaim the Pope, but millions do not listen to his truths and admonitions; nor do they obey him. Italy is in a sad state!

It is in a particularly bad situation because it has not responded, or sufficiently so, to all the tearful pleas of Mary made there in recent years. We have already mentioned her tearful complaints made through Father Gobbi who is home-based in the Milan archdiocese. And we have seen the outpouring of tears at Syracuse decades ago. We now take up many other alleged weepings.

Let me first mention in passing something else that is not a passing thing. Italy recently has had the first priest stigmatist in history, Padre Pio, and that for fifty years until he died in 1968. Italy at present has the well-known stigmatist, "Brother" Gino, who became a priest in 1983. Not long ago the nun stigmatist, Sister Elena Aiello died, and the laywoman stigmatist Teresa Musco. I was told just the other day on good authority that there is an elderly nun stigmatist in or near Rome.

These stigmatists have represented all facets of Catholic life and vocation in Italy. Let us not casually use the word "stigmatists". The plural means that a lot of blood has flowed from the wounds of Christ in these persons. There are other stigmatists not long deceased and others yet alive. As in the martyrs, Christ suffers, bleeds, sweats, weeps, sheds tears of blood, agonizes through them. Do not stigmatists then as persons have a unique, superior value in relation to statues? Yet Christ and Mary seem so desperate today that they weep at times and bleed even through their material images, even through stone. And they have wept and bled much through their images in Italy.

This author must point out here that he cannot go into details, nor give any decisions or possible comments of various Italian dioceses. Were he aware of any one "weeping" that has had a final authoritative condemnation he would not include such a site, or would at least note the case. If people do witness an elephant run down Main Street, it is reported as news if nothing else. If there are credible reports or "news" of various weepings, especially with unprejudiced and non-"hysterical" photos, this author still leaves final judgment, as always, to the ultimate, high Church authorities. Catholics are always expected to obey their local episcopal ordinaries.

Catholics, however, like everybody else, are entitled to the news. And in the present atmosphere of evading the supernatural in many places, and among many clerics, Catholics are confused at times as to the conclusiveness of some chancery investigations or episcopal opinions. True, individual bishops (and saints) have differed in their convictions about reported apparitions, revelations, etc. Such judgments concern matters open to corrections. Clarity, however, would be a blessing!

So we shall, practically speaking, list only chronologically these claimed weepings with an explanatory word or two. We are not even sure we include them all, for only recently we had information and striking photos of the images of the late Teresa Musco, whose sacred images account for several weepings of both ordinary tears and streams of *blood*. We shall conclude with Teresa's images later and with some amazing things in connection with Sister Elena Aiello.

If Italy has not had a great number of sorrowful and tear-full pleas and warnings from Christ and His Mother, then no nation, place or person has had them!

In his book, *Explosion of the Supernatural* we have noted that John Haffert, lay head of the famous Blue Army, of Our Lady, mentions alleged modern apparitions to the number of twenty, most of them apparently having occurred in Italy. Our listings, however, are not his.

Since 1940, apparitions have been reported at Balestrino, at Montichiari, 1947, at Cimigliano di Venarotta, 1948, at Marta, 1948, at Ulzio, 1967, and, already commented on, at San Damiano (beginning 1964). As far as the author can ascertain, there have been, at some time or other, unfavorable local ecclesiastical reports about all above except Ulzio. This does not necessarily mean conclusively so in all cases.

At Tre Fontane, Rome, 1947, Mary appeared in a grotto to several children and their Communist father, Bruno Cornacchiola. It is a shrine visited by many today and seems to have remained in good standing. Mary appeared there as "The Virgin of Revelation" and that seems an apt title for our days, especially in view of her later visitations and the Father Gobbi book.

To take up a number of claimed "weepings" (usually associated with apparitions also), a few years after the great weepings at Syracuse, others began in 1957 at Rocca Corneta in the diocese of Bologna. A statue of the Madonna with Child is claimed to have shed tears over 100 times, weeping up to two hours at a time. In 1972 also and apparently in 1975. Analysis showed human tears.

In 1957 also, at Trenzano, (Brescia), a Madonna is shown with blood tears streaming over her face with a cloth over her chest to catch it. A statue of the Sacred Heart is also shown weeping blood there May 24, 1957.

Beginning on January 3, 1971, at Maropati, diocese of Mileto, southern Italy, a picture of Our Lady of Pompeii (Rosary devotion) with the Dominican saints Dominic and Catherine, shed or wept tears of *blood*. It is owned by the respected lawyer John Baptist Cordiano. It started to weep January 3, 1971. Chemists and scientists are reported as saying that human blood tears flowed from the three images and formed crosses on the wall below the picture, before spectators. There are at least two post-cards — bloodied pictures!

Blood also came from Mary's heart, hands and feet. The blood ran intermittently, sometimes not showing for weeks. According to *Fatima International,* Msgr. Francesco Luzzi was reported as saying there was no doubt the facts occurred as the lawyer, Cordiano, has said. (The Monsignor was ordered by the Vatican to investigate.) Police and local officials supported the account. In 1973 this picture was again reported (in Canada) as having shed blood in 1972.

As in some other cases this image seems to present Mary (the Mother of Sorrows) as a "stigmatist". Certainly in her co-redemptive sufferings with and over her Son at the foot of the Cross, the Compassionate Mother of the Saviour suffered more than any stigmatist daughter or son of hers!

In 1972, as indicated earlier, there was an amazing additional number of images reported as weeping. I will list those in Italy alphabetically:

Near *Assisi* (this must be Porziano di Assis), a statue of Our Lady of Fatima was shedding tears. When a newspaper headlined: "It's truly becoming a bad habit; another statue weeping", it witnessed to more than it thought. Human tears on the cheek from the eye or eyes was reported elsewhere as occurring 28 of Gennaio (January) 1972.

In Cinquefrondi (Reggio Calabria) a Madonna was reported (in 1973) as "still weeping" in 1972.

In Lendinara (Adria-Rovigo) a picture of Our Lady of Sorrows in a frame at the place of the Olivetan Benedictine Fathers ("White Fathers") was reported as shedding tears. Another account placed a weeping image of the "Sacred Heart of Mary", which shed human tears 1st, February 1972, as occurring at Lendinara, presumably the same image.

Near Naples, a Canadian report of 1973 told of a picture, no details, that was shedding blood in 1972. (This may have been Maropati.)

At Porto San Stefano (Grosseto) there is a statue of Mary, Queen of the World, with a colored globe (of the earth) in her hands, in the home of Enzo Alocci, who seems to be a reputable seer, with many apparitions of Mary, beginning March 27, 1966. This significant statue of Mary, by title and posture, shed tears in 1972 on each day from July 3 through July 7, also July 11 and July 19.

Blood also flowed from Mary's eyes on October 16 and again in November on the first, seventeenth and eighteenth. Also blood on December 2, 6, and 20, 1972. My last report available, is that it shed blood tears again in 1973.

It seems the blood-tears fell on top of the globe and spread over it. Can there be a more dramatic, fearsome, and pleading message from the Queen of the World, and the Mother of the Church and of men? At any rate the symbolic message seemed that Mary, Queen of the World was shedding tears of blood over the world, *our* globe! Apparitions of Mary, the weepings and the seer all seem very authentic at Porto San Stefano, and very significant. (Incidentally, there is a Queen of the World statue before the *Domus Pacis*—House of Peace—of the Blue Army at Fatima.)

Ravenna has been already mentioned by Mary herself to Father Gobbi, regarding her weeping statue and her own tears. I presume this is the same Fatima statue that wept human tears December 9, 1972 and has been photographed with some on the chin.

At Vertora (Bergamo) a Madonna with a sword in her heart is said to have shed blood-tears from her eyes in 1972.

We will comment more later on what seems to be behind this flood of human salt-tears and those of blood in Italy in 1972, particularly by relating it to a Jacinta of Fatima warning, and, to a U.S. seer's statements in 1972-3. And to some prophecies of Sister Elena Aiello!

After simply listing all these reported apparitions and/or weepings I believe the reader can see the impossibility, in this book, of going into details. Large volumes at times are written about single cases of alleged apparitions, private revelations, weepings, etc. If any of these apparitions or cryings have proven unauthentic, or will be, I am sure an impressive number will remain; and that more research and knowledge would bring out more apparent "supernatural" signs and communications, especially the more private and hidden ones, and those kept secret sometimes even until the deaths of the privileged souls.

Need I recall, that a prophetic "cartoon" or picture-composite from one of a group of little seers in Sicily (the cartoon is still existent), depicted Italy being overturned, and another such "picture" in 1972, showed Italy being transversed with blood.

Elsewhere we have referred to Sister Elena of Italy (Calabria) and some very sobering communications from Christ and Mary. We again report here briefly on an unusual "image" — it was that of Christ's face in agony appearing bloodily on panelling near Sister Elena's bed, with blood running down the panel from the miraculously imposed image.

I have not been able to ascertain whether Teresa Musco said anything about Mary's tears or saw Mary weep or say anything. I am merely listing weepings of images in Teresa's home at Caserta, Italy. The information is taken from large, magnificent, colored photos given to me by an Italian priest interested in promoting Teresa's canonization cause. Teresa was a stigmatist and died only in *1976*. Again, significantly, these many weepings, and some bloody, took place *near Rome* and fairly recently. (Recently another worthy Italian priest told me that Teresa saw Christ and Mary weeping or bleeding when their images became animated.)

If one had detailed weepings, the natural salt and blood tears of all the reported images above, one could well see how Italy from top to bottom has been drenched with the vicarious weepings of Mary. It represents a great effort on Mary's part to plead for hope by a change of heart in men, while at the same time warning what grievous trials and tribulations can happen to her sinful children.

We now take up the Teresa Musco images and it will be convenient to include here those of Christ, and yes, a final appeal of final dramatic appeals, that of the Bambino or Infant Jesus weeping.

These facts are taken directly from information on the amazingly graphic photos of images in the home of Teresa Musco.

The Marian statue in Teresa Musco's home, which was photographed in color in a number of weepings, is a lovely one of the Immaculate Conception type, white clothing with large blue sash, rosary on right arm, and folded hands pointing upwards, and her eyes (which seem to be dark or hazel brown) raised heavenwards. A nimbus of twelve stars rings Mary's head.

This statue first began weeping on December 8, 1975, and the last reported weeping I am aware of was August 15, 1976. There is one photo-card with a sequence of six pictures of the statue weeping blood, from the initial tears in both eyes to the blood running down her cheeks and throat.

Photographed weepings of this statue:

March 12, 1976, about 3:40 p.m., one picture with one regular tear suspended from the chin; one picture with two tears there.

Sunday, March 21, 1976, about 2:30 p.m., blood from both eyes, a stream of blood running down the right cheek. The same day about 3:00 p.m., the stream from the right eye ends in a tear suspended from the chin.

Friday, April 2, 1976, at 4:35 p.m., blood tears from both eyes, with a stream-trickle down left cheek and a big tear on left chin. As in a few other instances, neck of statue (and/or cheek) seems to have traces of blood as if blood liquid had been wiped off.

Saturday, April 3, 1976, at 12:50 noon, blood from both eyes of "Mary" practically covering her face and showing vividly down her neck.

Same day, at about 1:30 p.m., blood all the way down her neck, and across neck-band of dress and on to white clothing.

Monday, May 10, 1976, from 3:40 p.m. to 4:30 p.m., bloody eyes, bloody even above them, blood on cheeks; two big tears on chin, trickles or remnants of blood down neck and on dress by her hands; and, apparently, some blood even below her folded hands on dress.

A Head of Christ in Agony near Teresa's bed, an "Ecce Homo!", showed reddened, bloody eyes; it wept, March 25, 1976, at 3:40 p.m.

A statue of the Sacred Heart of Jesus shed blood tears, June 3, 1976, at 3:35 p.m. Blood smears the fact and a red globule hangs suspended from the beard of Our Lord.

A crucifix in the house of Teresa also shed blood many times. The face and upper body of the Corpus was smeared with blood.

Finally, shockingly and shattering, two separate Bambinos, Infant images, as one looks upon lovingly in a Church Christmas Crib, have shed tears of blood, and in a copious manner. One of these weepings *(lacrimazioni)* of *Gesu Bambino* took place Saturday, May 22, at 3:30 p.m.

It is impossible to escape all this photographic evidence, and this in the home of a stigmatist, only a few years ago, not far from Rome. One may also ask, is it just an accident that the stigmatist, "Brother" Gino, lives only a short distance from Rome? And Enzo Alocci at Porto San Stefano is only an hour away by train.

A final picture of a blood-weeping elsewhere, is that of a statue of the Immaculate and Sorrowful Heart of Mary at Castel S. Lorenzo

(Salerno). It is a white statue with Mary holding out her hands. There is no blood from her eyes or on her face, but from her heart image, prominent on the front of her breast, a great amount of blood flows downwards and saturates the base of the statue; it falls upon what seems to be either a mass of cloth or cotton. Mary here too has a nimbus of stars, as does Teresa's Mary statue. This may suggest the Apocalyptic woman "clothed with the sun" and confronting the Dragon.

This is a very striking and "bloody" picture. The statue is reported as having wept blood many times.

Finally we have also heard of a weeping Virgin Mary image at Firenze (Florence) the city of Flowers, shedding blood.

And in 1972 the Fatima statue of "Brother" Gino, according to Father Ronald Tangen, in the shrine crypt at San Vittorino, also wept. Apparently because the Blessed Mother thought the building of the Fatima Shrine there, its full construction, should have been moving at a faster pace. The shrine is practically complete at this writing.

Which is just another way of Mary saying in 1972, that the Fatima Message was urgent.

The *Explosion* book says a statue also shed blood in Rome. Sister Elena has prophesied that Rome will be purified in blood.

A message from Padre Pio was printed in the *Soul* magazine, Nov-Dec. 1978. We quote in part:

"Let Marian groups of pious souls, in a spirit of reparation, organize pilgrimages to the sanctuaries of the Madonna, praying the Rosary together for God's mercy and pity. The Most Blessed Virgin, Compassionate Mother, who sheds tears of blood over today's world, calls all Her children to penance and prayer.

"Let these pilgrimages be made in a spirit of penance, and let the clothing of women be modest and simple, without vanity."

"And so I come here today because on this very day last year, in Saint Peter's Square in Rome, the attempt on the Pope's life was made, in mysterious coincidence with the anniversary of the first apparition at Fatima, which occurred on May 13, 1917." — John Paul II at Fatima. May 13, 1982.

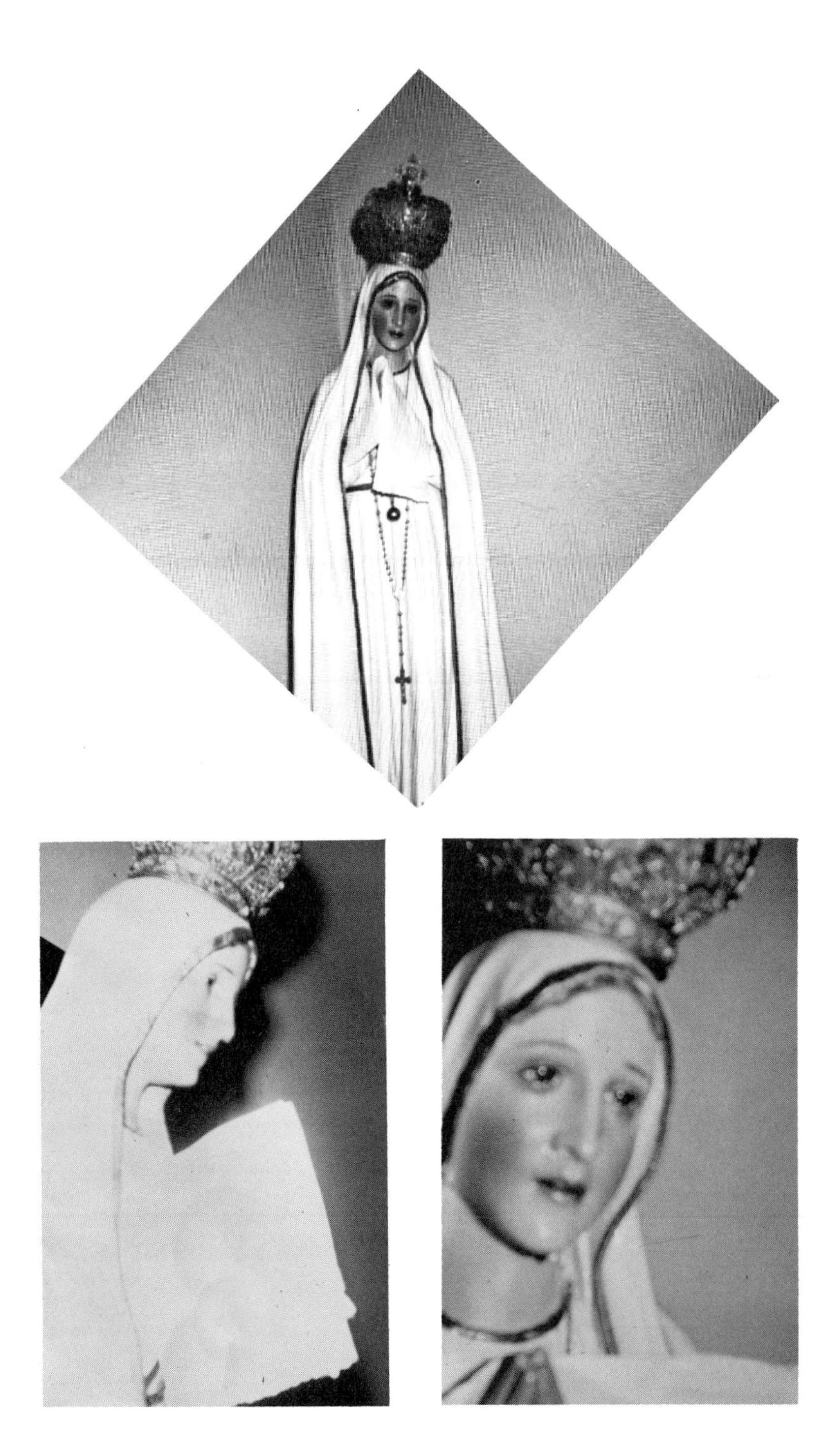

No. Am. Pilgrim Virgin weeping, New Orleans, July 1972

No. Am. Pilgrim Virgin weeping, Atlanta, July 21, 1972

Three images owned by "AW" that have wept, the Fatima statue many times.

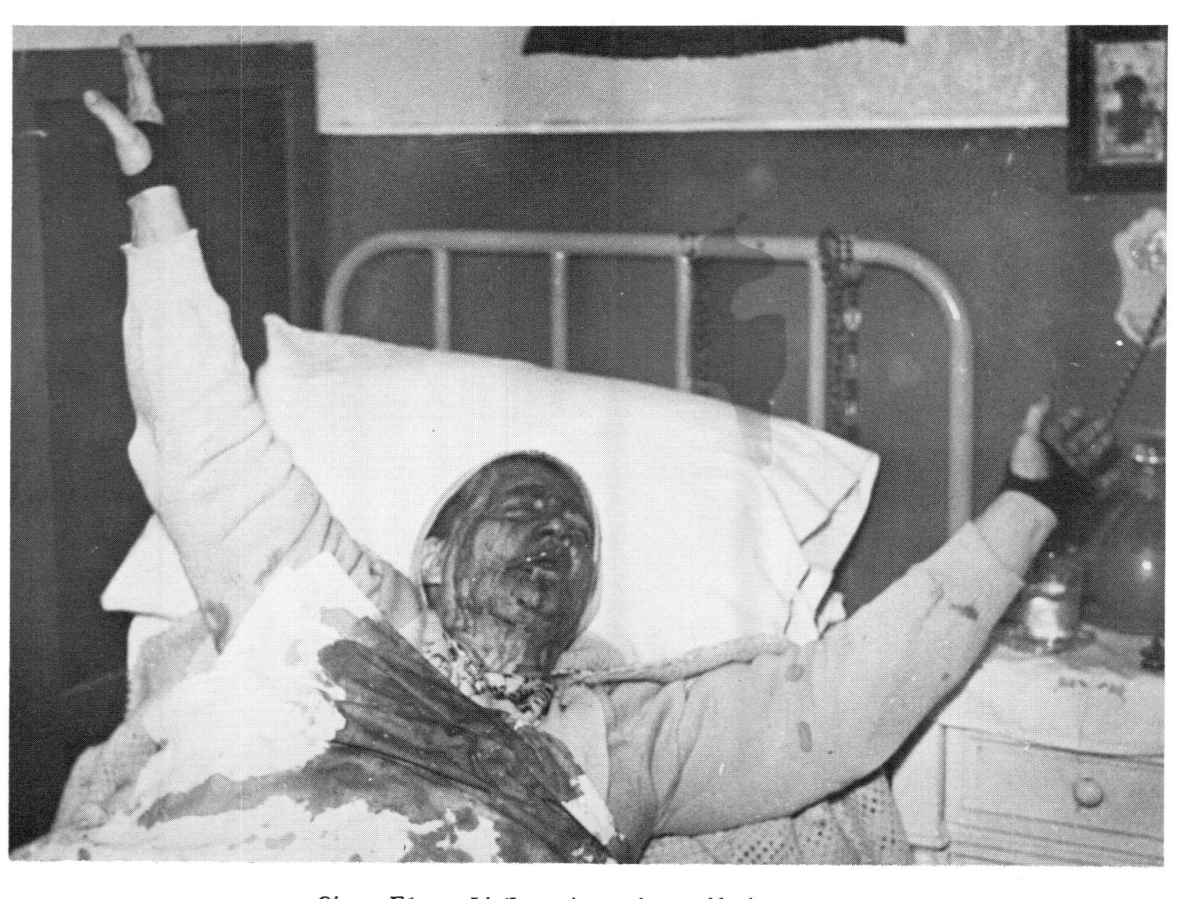

Sister Elena Aiello, stigmatist, suffering agony

Some persons expect a seer or "mystic" to have a "hot-line" to God and to be able to answer any question correctly, about the future, unknown things, etc. I have known "mystics" to have been asked questions like these: Is the stock-market going up for a particular stock; or, what was the date of a person's unknown birth-time?

Now, if such a seer could answer any question given by anyone in the world and always correctly, naturally all the leaders of the world, even presidents and popes would constantly question them. It simply does not work like that.

Even with saints, or future saints, and where they claim private revelations, prophecies, special messages for mankind, etc., discernment has to be made. It is not always easy, but *tears* are *objective* things. Tears not only have their own message for any witness, they confirm the authenticity of the accompanying "seer"; they call attention to the one claiming a mission and to the message of the claimant.

Famous mystics and saints have been mistaken at times, and fooled by the devil, by their own imagination or interpretations; or by imprudently asking questions the Lord would not answer, and where the devil or their own psychology supplied a false answer. Particularly so in the early stages of such a privileged soul's years, much discernment is needed to sift the true from the false and the good from the bad. An apparition or locution by itself might be in doubt, but objective tears cannot be, and in their miraculous presence confirm the credibility of the former and any *substantial* message content.

We forget, that when we read certain saints' lives or those so reputed, or those of "seers" and "mystics", particularly if the subject has been a Religious, or a woman closely guarded at home, that superiors, confessors or spiritual directors often have ordered them not to pass on or publicize particular things, such as individual locutions. Or those in responsible offices plainly told the "saint" or "seer" that he or she was wrong in certain instances or had been deceived.

Again, as is particularly so with women religious, Sisters, only years later we learn of the more certain private revelations. Church authorities themselves at times hold back certain elements of private revelations, as with Fatima, which they will eventually publish as credible (we do not mean to say the Third Secret will necessarily be published). But years are not needed to establish the reality of photographed and laboratory analyzed tears. Even restricted to themselves such tears speak a message more dramatic and appealing than words. My mother, or anyone else's mother may not speak words when she weeps, but her tears are in themselves a heart-striking message.

In the beginning of a seer's years of a mission in the open with unusual claims or manifestations, particularly for a layman or laywoman, and especially if the Church or certain members of the Church do not meet fully the responsibilities of discerning the facts or providing for spiritual direction (not dictation!), then there is more chance for some error's infiltration; and, naturally, more controversy than usual. But that does not affect what might be called the basic facts, the substantial revelations, and the overall credibility and real virtues of the person. *Tears* proclaim that *something* is there! *Look at the tears then,* consider the tears if nothing else. And *ponder their message.*

So, with "seers", "instruments", "victim souls", "prophets", and, yes, priests, other less favored people should be reasonable, and regard the important and vital things, the objective facts and the good fruits. Also, everyone always should be ready for submission to Church authorities, even if, temporarily, locally, such authorities may place restrictions they will lift later on.

But, beware lies and slanders, *a priori* prejudices, and comments by those not intimate with all the facts; or when decisions and judgments are made and statements given out without a supporting rationale; and without interviewing at length the main subject/s and principal or vital witnesses. The faithful are not unreasonable when they ask for a reasonable investigation into such important occurrences; a competent one and with a report of the facts, not mere declarations. Any condemnatory charge uttered by anyone against any alleged "seer" should be able to stand trial before a civil, criminal or ecclesiastical court of law. The eighth commandment demands it.

Saint Augustine would back up such procedures. He proclaimed passed-on miracles from his cathedral church at Hippo. He presented publicly the persons concerned. Augustine believed in the value of supernatural manifestations for strengthening the faith of the people. True, he confronted all sorts of errors, but he also presented all sorts of truths. Augustine was an outstanding Bishop, a great mind, a saint, a Father and Doctor of the Church.

> "Do not stifle the Spirit. Do not despise prophecies. Test everything; retain what is good. Avoid any semblance of evil." — 1 Th. 5:19-22

XI — SOME WEEPINGS IN THE UNITED STATES

"This time I say it with tears." **Phil. 3:18.**

In our own United States let me first mention, in this preliminary chapter, what seem to be a few lesser weepings, though they may not be that way with God. Even in writing about foreign-soil weepings, certain names have been kept secret as with "Marguerite" and the Hungarian mother.

Surprisingly so, any claimed "seers" in European territory, especially non-Iron Curtain, can quickly be beset by "pilgrims", plagued by the curious, or insulted by skeptics, even from far-off lands. To give their names and addresses away, unless they so desire or confirm that their mission is open to publicity as to its source (or their home) seems utterly unfair to their right to some private life and/or family duties and unity.

Such interference and harassment has occurred in the cases of several United States "mystics" known to the author and whom he personally believes to be authentic seers. So names will be avoided and exact locations in all cases. Any responsible persons wishing to communicate with this author over important matters, such as reference to back-up affidavits, may do so; but this author will not get involved with trite matters of curiosity, unbelief or controversy. He is asking sincere people to look at *facts of weepings* and to draw their own conclusions.

That is the important thing here and now, and not meeting "seers", being curious, moving in on a chosen soul's life, wanting to see a weeping or to know in detail many other associated wonders at times, such as private revelations, cures or unusual knowledge. That is too big a task to handle here. Our motto, rather, is "a picture (or its description for the absent) is worth 20,000 words."

Let this author observe that he has been informed about, or made aware of any number of alleged "miraculous" or supernatural incidents or happenings: "tears", images on doors or windows, images in the sky, unusual photos, "spinning suns", smiles of statues, movements of statues, etc. He has disregarded practically all of these, though, certainly, some were probably genuinely inexplicable by natural causes.

Concerning others, perhaps, some enduringly true, it has been impossible, because of time, geography and other reasons, to pursue the matter. So he will not mention "negative" cases, but a few that seem credible; he speaks here however of *lesser* incidents only when compared to the big sequences of weepings we shall shortly review.

So the *Register*, national Catholic weekly, reported a supposedly miraculous image on the wall of an unused convent near Holman, New

Mexico. Archbishop Robert F. Sanchez of Santa Fe, however, spoke very cautiously about it then. Later he affirmed to this author that, "The reported image about 'tears' was false. Other unusual manifestations were simply images of nature."

I know a lady in the Eastern United States (not any well-known "Seer"), who claims her statue of the Immaculate Conception, which a bishop blessed for her, wept. I know another lady in the Massachusetts area who had a statue of Our Lady of Fatima that she claims, turned blue. As she was a good sensible woman in important religious activities, such as promoting adoration of the Eucharist, and this was a private confidence I have no reason to doubt her. Additionally I know of several priests (two nationally known) concelebrating together in the eastern United States who witnessed a famous statue of Our Lady of Fatima turn blue during a Mass.

I have heard a reliable report that a Marian image in the care of a Christian (but Orthodox) Faith, in a Byzantine church, wept some time ago in New York State. But I definitely have a news item (and photo) story of the icon painting of Saint Nicholas reported as weeping Christmas morning a few years ago at the Greek Orthodox church at Tarpon Springs, Florida. Reportedly, thousands streamed in for days to see the tears. Father Elias Kalariotes was reported as telling the capacity congregation at the Christmas morning liturgy service that the tears were being shed for the sins of the world, of mankind.

From a responsible source I have a report of a statue of Saint Therese of Lisieux, the Little Flower, weeping in the home of a New England lady, and that it has bled. Cures are reported. But I would not give out the lady's address. People can accept or reject the report as they will.

I know of another lady in a small town in a Southern state with a statue of Mary reported as weeping. I have spoken with two reliable women in the New Orleans metropolitan area whose personal statues have wept, one of which statues was of Our Lady of Fatima and which wept several times.

More, I know of claims made by a Rosary and Sacred Heart enthronement "apostle" of Our Lady of Fatima, that a Fatima statue (or statues circulated in homes) in part of a certain southern state, has (or have) wept several times. And I recall another Fatima statue in the Columbus, Ohio area that wept.

No doubt such claims and real happenings, more often of a private nature, could be multiplied. It would be difficult to measure, however, the total impact of such local weepings in various sections of the United States.

In the press recently, a second International Fatima Pilgrim Virgin statue has been reported as weeping in the United States. We shall mention these two weepings (important because of the nature of the statue) before going into more famous and frequent weepings of special Fatima statues in the United States, including the first International Pilgrim Virgin statue of 1947 to North America.

This second International Fatima statue (it has been called the "European" statue) had been touring the United States for several years. (It has since been recalled by the Bishop of Fatima and the original North American International Pilgrim Virgin statue recalled from South America to the United States.) This second statue was not the one that wept at New Orleans in 1972 which was the original Pilgrim Virgin of 1947 to North America.

This second statue was first in the United States on June 23, 1974. It is four feet tall and made of Brazilian cedar wood. It has been blessed by several popes, including Pope John Paul II. This statue was originally blessed in May, 1947 to tour Europe. On August 5, 1959, when the helicopter pilot hovered over Padre Pio's cell at San Giovanni Rotondo, Italy with the statue, Padre Pio was cured of a lengthy illness.

Both the Las Vegas *Sun* and the magazine *Soul* reported this statue as weeping in that city in January, 1978. The *Sun* article said that as many as 6,000 southern Nevadans, including Mayor Bill Briare of Las Vegas, saw the statue weep.

"During the statue's January 8-19 visit", former radio broadcaster Don Jaye said, "it was observed weeping in five different locations on three different days." This author has a personal letter and a statement as to this weeping from Mayor Briare. And affidavits of others!

One interpretation is that Mary was weeping over the legalization of prostitution in a number of counties in Nevada. Personally, it would seem to this author, such a publicized weeping or weepings of a famous Fatima statue with a special and important mission, would have much larger significance. Also these weepings called attention to the Fatima statue a little while before its worldwide "Queen of the World" tour took it to many lands not long afterwards.

This was the Fatima statue that was refused entry into Poland with a Communist general blocking it. A wire replica was made of it and carried around Poland. It would seem that Our Lady of Fatima wanted the world to be reminded again of her tears. There seems no doubt of the special significance of the statue's weeping for the "Sin-City" of Las Vegas.

Perhaps it wept also anticipating that Poland through a Communistic government would reject the Mother of the Land.

In its July August 1981 issue *Soul* magazine ran two pictures of this Pilgrim Virgin statue with "tears" in her eyes taken on May 4, 1980, in Carthage, New York. This author has heard from a person close to the statue, who should know, that the Las Vegas weepings (or perhaps one?) were only out of the right eye of the statue, which was considered an "extra" miracle, and that the Carthage weeping was from the *left* eye only. The pictures in *Soul,* one must observe, are not nearly as clear or striking for lacrimation effects as are tears in several photos of other weeping statues in this author's possession. One month later, on June 5, 1980 another Fatima statue in the metropolitan area of New Orleans, privately owned, began a series of weepings with some remarkable photos taken of the tears.

But let such reports of varied weepings in the United States introduce us to the further reality of very striking and extensive Fatima statue weeping sequences in America (U.S.), mainly concerning:

1) The original North American International Pilgrim Virgin statue of 1947;

2) The Fatima statue of a particular lady;

3) The Fatima statues of a particular man.

"*Madonna mia!* The day you arrived in Italy I became sick. Now you are leaving, and you leave me like this . . ." — Padre Pio when cured as Pilgrim Virgin statue left.

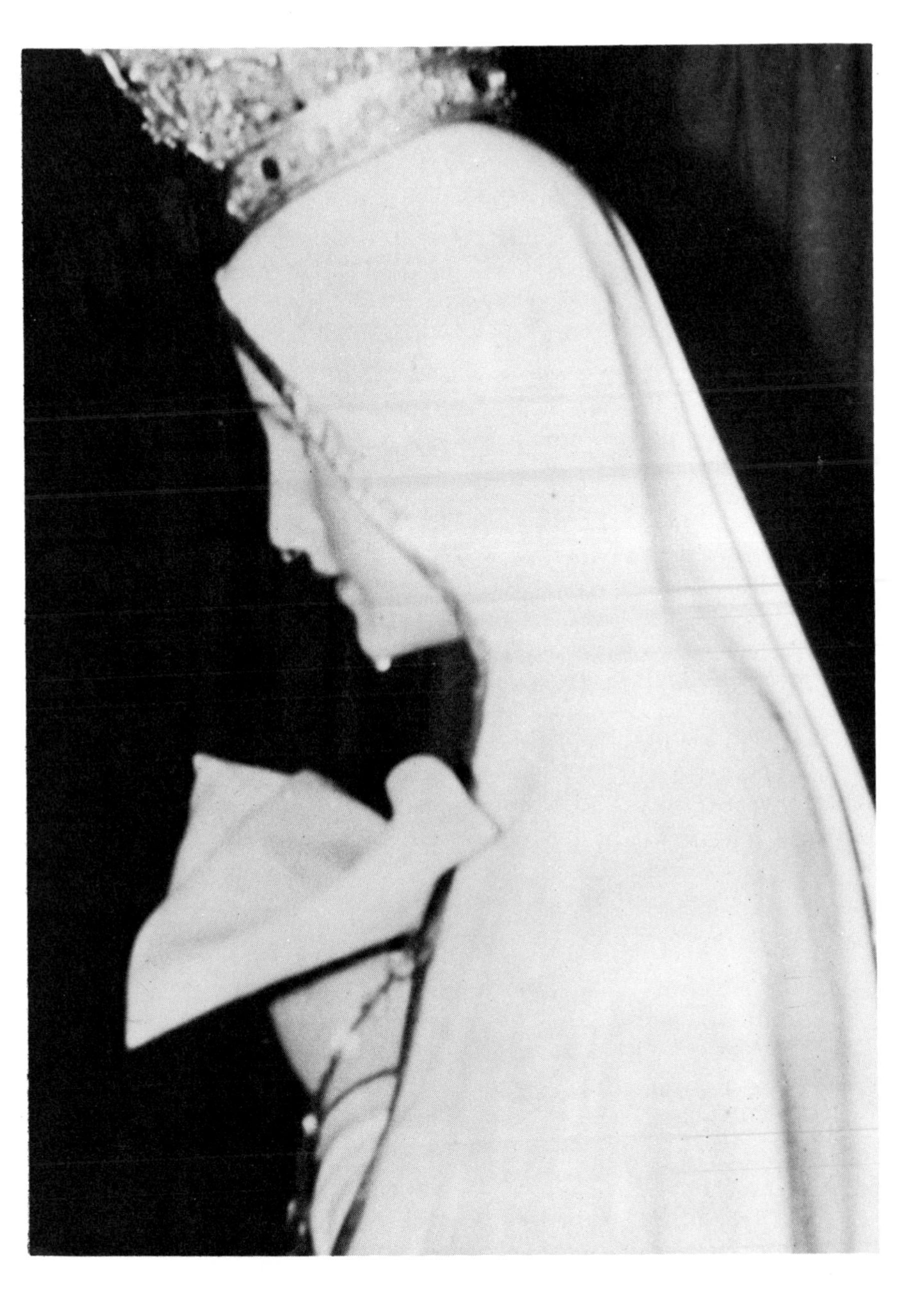

North American Pilgrim Virgin, June 14, 1972

XII — TWO FAMOUS WEEPING FATIMA STATUES IN UNITED STATES

***"Let my eyes stream with tears day and night."* Jer. 14:17.**

A — *The International Pilgrim Virgin Statue*

In July, 1972 the United States based International Fatima Pilgrim Virgin statue, blessed for North America in 1947, came to New Orleans. It had originally arrived in Canada after having been blessed by the Bishop of Leiria, Portugal (Fatima diocese), and was then received in the United States with great enthusiasm at Buffalo, New York. The blessing at Fatima took place, October 13, 1947 in the presence of some 250,000 pilgrims there. By 1972 it had visited innumerable dioceses and archdioceses in the United States and Canada, had been venerated by millions of people, and all sorts of physical cures and spiritual graces had been reported.

This Fatima statue had been carved by the famous sculptor, Jose Ferreira Thedim, out of cedarwood, under the direction of Lucy, the surviving seer of the three children of the Fatima apparitions in 1917. The image had the glass or "crystal" eyes common to such statues. This famous Fatima statue, which served as the "Ambassador" image of Our Lady of Fatima, from the Shrine of Fatima itself, was then (at New Orleans) under the supervison of its third priest-custodian.

The statue's original custodian had been Monsignor William C. McGrath, P.A., who preached with it for about twenty years. He was also well-known for his book, *Fatima or World Suicide*. Monsignor McGrath died July 13, 1970. In accordance with the policy of the author, names of custodians connected with the statue after Monsignor McGrath, and with its weepings, will be withheld, as also other later guardians or escorts after August 6, 1972.

A certain lady, "AW", our subject here, acted as secretary for arranging tours of the statue. The third custodian of the statue was also her spiritual director. This lady was an exile from Poland or the former free city state of Danzig (Gdansk) because of persecution by the Communists after they occupied Poland. In America she gave lectures on Communism and its evils, and on Fatima and its message. She believed, because of an unusual incident in her childhood, which had no meaning for her many years, that she had a mission of renewal within the Church.

It is not our purpose to go into these claims here, although this author believes they are well-backed up. One, however, might note the unusual situation of someone claiming a mission associated with the *Fatima* message, who, far from her native Poland, became closely associated with the International Virgin statue *from Fatima to North America.* Also, that this famous and important Fatima Mission ambassadorial statue would have a number of important weepings in her presence. We must remember that this statue was blessed at Fatima by its Bishop, October 13, 1947 (anniversary of the sun miracle), to bring the *Fatima message* to North America.

When the said Pilgrim Virgin statue came to New Orleans in July, 1972, it was learned then at the Crescent City that it had wept a number of times before, but without national publicity. These prior weepings should be noted as belonging to two classifications of cryings, the first and early group of tear-sheddings that would seem more or less at random and largely for the benefit of individuals. Then, a later series of weepings were closely associated with the lady's presence, the lady we have designated as "AW".

We will note than that the Pilgrim Virgin statue had wept a good dozen times before coming to New Orleans. As a pastor in Agawam, Massachusetts, wrote to the *Clarion Herald* of New Orleans after the July, 1972 weepings there: "You can quote me, I have seen real tears rolling down the cheeks of the statue." Once, in Connecticut, its tears spilled over a small boy's tee shirt. The priest with the statue, at that time the second Custodian, cut out a portion of the wet shirt as something "precious". In passing, we might note that cures have been attributed to the use of or application of such tear-wetted cloths.

Upon another occasion a man was doing some touch-up work on the statue (at times people have caressed and smeared it). When its tears fell upon him, as he worked in a home basement, he looked up thinking it was from the plumbing or something above. It was the Pilgrim Virgin crying.

Significantly, as we indicated, this weeping took place in the home of the above lady who acted as secretary for its tours or appearances, and at whose home at times the statue was left when not circulating on its "pilgrimage" visitations. This happened about 1971 and was one of the weepings that showed a transition period in the weeping phenomena of the statue. It was weeping more and more markedly at the home or in the presence of this lady.

For instance, at the time of the Attica Prison riot, September, 1971, the Pilgrim Virgin statue wept at this lady's home. Reportedly there was a message at the time from Mary: "See how mankind treats his fellowman!" This same Pilgrim Virgin statue wept at the time of the Rapid City Flood, June, 1972. It wept again at the lady's home, July 3, 1972.

One might have asked then, what were these weepings leading to, to what matters were they linked, and why especially associated with a person claiming a special renewal mission?

If the Pilgrim Virgin did weep to call attention to a flood disaster (242 died at Rapid City), and to a prison massacre (42 died at Attica), her tears up to that point seemed directed more to individuals or small groups for their spiritual enlightenment, "conversion", or the energizing of apostolates, such as that for Eucharistic adoration. But pertinent witnesses of the tears were to increase and also *professional photos.*

The same Pilgrim Virgin statue (we said it indirectly already) once turned blue in the presence of three priests in New York State. That temporary change was taken as a sign to confirm the undertaking of a certain spiritual commitment. Such a happening and changes in the expression of statues are not isolated. A good lady living in the eastern United States, active in adoration work, claimed, as noted above, that her Fatima statue once turned blue. Also, as we recall, the *Regina Mundi* (Queen of the World) statue of Enzo (Porto San Stefano, Italy) turned all blue then remained blue except for the cloak.

But to get to the more famous, photographically recorded and "final" weepings of the International Pilgrim Virgin, — "final", at least as far as this author can determine, for a long period, if not to date, that is from August 5, 1972. (This author has inquired and written in vain to establish otherwise.)

In New Orleans by Sunday, July 16, 1972, the International Pilgrim Virgin statue had completed its main engagements. It was then kept at the rectory of a certain church (A) which had frequent Adoration of the Blessed Sacrament services. But the lady, who had arrived the day before by car with her four children from New York State, and who had given a lecture at that church the same evening, sent word that the statue should be in her room (315) at the Ramada Inn on Tulane Avenue, where she was staying with her children.

The Pilgrim Virgin statue wept in her room that Monday evening, July 17, 1972. This author has heard, in his presence, two reliable witnesses of that weeping so attest to it. Another witness, an editor-photographer stated that at the drying-out time of the tears he touched the still wet eyes with his finger; camera shots of the tear clearly visible to all, at the tip of his little finger, were made.

The next morning, in the same room, the statue began weeping about four a.m. This weeping was spread over hours, and famous photos of it (photos this author believes absolutely authentic) went around the world through the Associated Press service. The lady at the night-desk of the motel witnessed it, the janitor witnessed it, and some ladies were called who came to witness it.

As we have said, we are dealing with facts here. I quote from a sworn affidavit: "I sat in a chair . . . just watching what transpired. For two and a half hours that I watched, liquid rose in the statue's eyes to full capacity, then rolled down the crevices parallel to her nose, into her teeth and mouth, also curving down the nose to the tip swelling into a large tear and then dropping onto the altar napkin covering her hands. Also flowing to the tip of the chin likewise becoming a large droplet and falling to the cloth."

From another affidavit we have another adult reaction to the same weeping of the Pilgrim Virgin statue at New Orleans: "There She was with the tears in her eyes. I looked into Her face. She had a very sad but beautiful look on Her face. I thought and asked Her, what could I do to stop the tears, what could I say to console Her. . . . But it didn't stop then. . . . After several hours had passed, more or less, since my arriving, I noticed the tears in Her eyes were drying."

Another statement declares that two registered nurses "gathered the 'tear' on a sterile slide . . . to have a pathological test made . . . with the results being of 'saline content and human origin'."

"Why Her tears!" was the question put in many papers and places as the photos and story of the weepings were published. This question was also asked by many people.

The "why" was given by the lady in a message statement to the Catholic Press, locally. Whatever the reason, it was not published although the picture and story of the weeping were published. In a word, the world missed the message that was apparently intended to circulate the earth with the story of the weepings and the photos.

One can only note that this Marian image was probably the then currently most famous statue in the world, the Ambassador Pilgrim Virgin Fatima statue to North America from Fatima itself, with its "reputation" greatly built up by its repeated weepings. Obviously it wept so often to call attention to something. That something happened at New Orleans with copious tears. The tears confirmed a message and the message explained the vicarious tears of Our Lady of Fatima, the Blessed Mother Herself.

Only days later, at Atlanta, Georgia, Friday, July 21, 1972, at the Holiday Suwanee Inn, the same Pilgrim Virgin statue wept in the motel room of the same lady, in that largely non-Catholic area. Non-Catholic newspaper people published photos and stories in the Atlanta *Constitution* and the Atlanta *Journal,* the great Southern city's prestigious metropolitan newspapers. Part of the message then given out, modified suitably for a largely non-Catholic audience, was published.

One Atlanta paper's Religion Editor stated: "Fluid that flows like tears does indeed flow from the brown eyes of the wooden Pilgrim Statue of Fatima." The photographer who accompanied that editor said: "We were with the statue some forty-five minutes and during that time we definitely saw 'moisture' in her eyes that to both of us resembled tears!"

After the weeping at Atlanta, the Pilgrim Virgin statue wept at the home of the lady secretary on Saturday evening, August 5, 1972, in New York State. As at New Orleans and at Atlanta there were professional photos taken of the tears.

A business executive witness to that weeping in the lady's New York home stated in an affidavit: "I observed that moisture was welling from the lower portion of both eyes, over the lower lids, travelling downwards alongside the nose and forming droplets on the tip of the nose. Also drops were forming on the point of the chin."

A teen-ager high-school boy also witnessed then: "There were flood-lights on it as a photographer took pictures. I could see moisture filling the eyes and on the nose and chin, even though I was about eight feet away. I thought how strange this seems, seeing a miracle in a modern suburban home. Then all I could think of was that I would do anything for Her if She would stop crying. Then we all knelt down and said a Hail Mary." There are other affidavits. This author has seen a number of photos of the tears shed on that occasion.

After the New York weeping above, the very next day, the lady was separated from the statue because its custodian went to Europe, and the statue was entrusted to other hands. In that transition, or after it, one must point out two major facts. The North American International Pil-grim Virgin statue that had wept so much, so often in the lady's presence, and which had wept *before* becoming associated with her, *stopped* weep-ing, even though it was kept in circulation. But the lady very shortly after the transfer received gifts of new Marian statues (one in August, one in September) which *did weep,* one of which was a *Fatima* statue which would become famous for its many weepings.

B — *The Immaculate Conception Statue and the Second Famous Fatima Image*

As noted above, the relationship of the lady from Danzig with the International Fatima Pilgrim Virgin statue terminated on Sunday, August

6, 1972, feast of the Transfiguration. Within less than two weeks the same lady was given an Immaculate Conception Lourdes statue along with a Christ the King statue by friends, a doctor and his wife. This was on Saturday, August 19, 1972.

This statue wept the next day, Sunday morning, August 20, 1972. This author knows of a venerable priest, credited with charismatic gifts, who described the weeping that day as being just like that of a woman weeping. This beautiful statue, with blue sash and with many pink roses about Our Lady's feet, wept on August 20, 1972, August 31, 1972 and other times thereafter, for a total of eight times, Tears on the statue's dress were tasted as salty. At one weeping two beautiful tears hung on the chin for about a half-hour.

There is no question of humidity or other unfortunate (and at times ridiculous) allegations of natural casualty! The matching Christ the King statue (a companion gift), of similar make, when right beside the weeping Immaculate Conception statue, did not weep. No question of deception! The lady has been willing (as at New Orleans) for any statue associated with her, that has wept, to be scientifically but respectfully examined. Nor can anyone get around the many weepings and competent witnesses of weepings at length of statues associated with the lady. The two Fatima statues especially have wept continuously and in the open in the presence of witnesses.

Amazingly, at the time of these weepings of the Immaculate Conception-Our Lady of Lourdes statue, the lady said she would receive a *Fatima* statue that would weep.

On September 12, 1972, a little over one month from the last weeping of the International Pilgrim Virgin statue at her home, and a shorter time from the weepings of the Immaculate Conception statue, the lady received a beautiful cedarwood Fatima statue from friends, another doctor and his wife. While in their possession for about two years, this statue from Portugal had never wept. But this Fatima statue did weep at the home of the lady on the day of its reception.

Moreover, the lady's new Fatima statue continued to weep, often, and at times copiously. Some of the dates were September 13, September 20, and September 21, 1972, with weepings as long as two and a half hours. Whatever the interpretation given, no one can escape the facts of these many weepings, with numerous witnesses and a number of statements or sworn affidavits by competent witnesses. Later there were newspaper and TV reports.

For instance, in Washington, D.C., on the morning of October 29, 1972, the Fatima statue wept in the hotel room of the lady with a well-known mystical theologian present who has testified to the fact. It was weeping in her room when several persons (including an FBI man) came to pick up the statue to take it to Gaston Hall of Georgetown University.

Before the lecture the lady was to give at 3:00 p.m. in Gaston Hall, when the lady was not near the statue, a nun noticed that it was weeping. That audience was estimated between 800 and 1,000 and many saw the statue weeping. We shall get back to the apparent significance of this weeping in Washington, D.C. in a minute.

Remember, in the week following the one when this Fatima statue was received and its initial weepings, within one 24 hour period three separate weepings of that Fatima statue totalled over six hours of crying. A man who witnessed a crying in a Long Island motel stated:

"The tears welled up in the eyes just like a human's tears do. Also the eyes looked so real, so much like actual eyes of a human being that when I looked into them, it was like looking right into a person's eyes. The tears were running down the cheeks . . ." The man, knowing what he saw but not just whom the statue represented, referred to the statue as "Fatima weeping". Perhaps he hit closer than he thought!

Let us review the facts again, before hearing of a brief but pertinent message claimed by the lady as coming from Mary. First, we have an entire series of weepings of the International Fatima Pilgrim Virgin statue to North America, and at a certain stage in 1971 and 1972 these weepings switch over, as it were, to special weepings in the presence of a certain lady. Then the tears burst, as it were, into great weepings at New Orleans, Atlanta and New York, the last three cryings photographed by professional photographers. Further, an important message was given, and all this within a period of only three weeks.

Then, only two weeks later, in a sort of transition period, we find the Immaculate Conception statue weeping a number of times in the home of the same lady. (We note *Fatima* is associated with the *Immaculate* Heart of Mary.) (And Lourdes with private revelations.)

We also find that the North American International Pilgrim Virgin Fatima statue has stopped weeping, despite such a string of weepings before it was associated with the lady, and after being associated with her. When this famed Fatima statue was separated from her, to put it simply and plainly, it stopped weeping. An apparent "instrument" of Our Lord and Our Lady was absent or removed from the statue, and a remarkable endorsing sign, tears, were not being shed by that Fatima statue. Apparently no special "instrument" was there to be endorsed.

Then, about five weeks after the last weeping of the International Pilgrim Virgin statue in her New York home, her own *Fatima statue* (the gift) begins to weep and continues to weep in an amazing sequence of cryings, including big American cities, starting with Washington, D.C., the national capital of the most powerful nation on earth. We cannot overstress the fact that the first big-city weeping (or weepings) took place before a large Catholic audience in the political and governmental center of the United States where diplomatic representatives from all over the world had their ambassadorial lodgings. What happened to the news media? Why did it not hit the wires of the world and the ambassadorial faces of the nations at their Monday morning coffee?

In this framework, both of complexity and a simple sequence of tear marvels, we also have the fact that the lady stated on September 20, 1972, at the time of several long weepings of her Fatima statue, that she had a message from the Virgin Mary. It said:

"I will keep on shedding tears in your presence until the world listens to the message I have given through you . . ."

In a real sense the world "heard" at Washington, D.C., yet it did not hear; it did not listen, when it could have been so easy to hear, so easy to listen. — We shall see something of this message later.

During that same period of many weepings, the Blessed Mother reportedly said to the lady: "I have buried them in signs!" — All very understandable!

In the presence of the facts of such signs, Mary's tears, *many* repeated vicarious tears, any good mystical theologian would accept the visible signs as backing up the message. It is not our intent to go into that here, or many other unusual factual things suggesting the authenticity of the claims that could be brought in here. We would need a big book just to describe facts of the physical weepings, more so to detail other wonders, and to print the many affidavits on hand in full that proclaim numerous tears.

With these things in mind let us note a dramtic sign, it would seem, at the time of the October 29, 1972 Washington 3:00 p.m. lecture and public weeping. On the same weekend that the lady's Fatima statue wept before so many witnesses at Georgetown University, and before a well-known mystical theologian and other persons separately, the original North American International Pilgrim Virgin statue was the center of attraction at a major Marian rally at the National Shrine of the Immaculate Conception, with bishops present.

On this big occasion, with the famous Fatima statue the center of attention at the National Shrine of Mary, after having wept so often in the past, one might have expected the Pilgrim Virgin to weep then — but it did not!

We can only comment that a famous and a very important Fatima statue did not weep where the lady was not present, although previously it had wept often where she was. But where the lady was present in the same city, the nation's capital, a second *Fatima* statue did weep, at least twice in one day, her own, a statue that had been weeping since first being in her presence.

More than one person has made very logical comments about where the finger of the Blessed Virgin pointed at Washington, or where her tears did. It pointed to a message, to endorse an instrument claiming and proclaiming a certain message! Otherwise nothing would seem to make sense, and we are dodging both human faith and reason. As a Doctor of Philosophy at a Catholic university said, when learning there had been a message at the New Orleans weeping, "that makes sense"; but such a sign without some message would make God look "stupid".

At New Orleans, the message could have gone around the world with the photos of tears, but did not. At Washington, considering the words reportedly from Mary quoted above, it was no accident that a Fatima statue, already and so quickly "established" by long weepings, wept again and before so many and prominent people. That the weeping occurred in the capital of the most powerful nation on earth, one in danger from atheistic Communism and Soviet Russia, was hardly incidental. Fatima, its world-affecting message, Russia and the United States are all intimately connected.

Here again, human means, agents, failed to spread the story of a weeping (tears no one could deny) and the message the tears backed. The media should have spread it over the United States and the world. Mary weeps in the capital of the greatest nation in the world through a Fatima statue! Fatima with all its prophetic warnings of vital importance to the whole human race. And the national press overlooks the story with all its dramatic elements!

Prudence may be a virtue and should be exercised, but Catholics (we hear so much of the "adult Catholic" able to listen with open mind — at times to near heretics!) have a right to the news; and to a bit of thinking about objective facts. What sort of being is not moved by tears? Especially by tears of his or her mother? Do we not have all sorts of experiences every day that we do know involve objective happenings? But few hit us with the real impact of someone crying, someone *dear* to us, someone eminently sane and repeatedly crying. We speak of Mary's vicarious tears.

We must briefly note here that many "seers", mystics, saints, stigmatists, etc., have been ignored, misunderstood, slandered, persecuted, even put under wraps and restrictions for years. We must look, however, through the clouds of confusion, rumors, lies, machinations of the devil and human weaknesses to get at the big and obvious facts. It is the truth that will make us free.

After the dramatic weepings in the Nation's capital the lady's own Fatima statue continued to weep. It wept in rural areas of New York and Pennsylvania.

It wept in Chicago, April 17, 1973, as a man witnessed, "gazing in awe, at the tears coming from her right eye, down the right cheek, and coming next to her nose, the tears proceeding down to her mouth, then to her chin, moistening the tip of her chin. At seeing this miracle I knelt down to say a Hail Mary, feeling a great peace within me, an inner joy this world cannot give." He adds, "these tears definitely tasted salty."

To that same weeping a Chicago doctor's wife witnessed: "I saw the tears trickling down . . . They placed Kleenex on her hands first (to catch the tears), and then Charles told the housekeeper to get a napkin and they used it."

The lady's statue wept at Pittsburgh, May 17, 1973. We hear from a woman, a Catholic lay leader: "I saw tear after tear drop from the eye to the nose, to the chin and to the handkerchief. I looked around once and said, 'I guess I am a doubting Thomas' and put my forefinger right under a tear on the chin and touched it to my lips and it was salty-tasting."

"People of the Cardinal's entourage (Cardinal Slipyj) — he had a suite on the same floor — also witnessed the weeping, including his Bishop-secretary, priests and laity of the Ukranian rite. I estimate about thirty persons altogether while I was present. I estimated the weeping time about four and a half hours or so." — Can anyone get around a four and a half hours Fatima statue weeping? Openly, and with continual access to many people?

The Fatima statue of the lady wept again at Pittsburgh, October 30, 1973, including Frankie Gustine the ballplayer claimed among the witnesses. It wept again in Chicago later. It wept in Wheeling, West Virginia, October 22, 1973, and the North American Pilgrim Virgin statue, touring in that area at the same time, did not.

The lady's Fatima statue continued to weep and weep, some weepings private, some of a more public nature. The lady has estimated — years ago! — the total cryings to have reached more than fifty. A Swiss journalist saw it weeping Saturday and Sunday, May 25-26, 1974, and took pictures of the last. After a period of quietude the lady's Fatima statue wept in 1981 at the times of the assassination attempts on the President's and on Pope John Paul II's life.

This Fatima statue has also smiled, has been fragrant, and has assumed various facial expressions such as moving its lips.

One could continue quoting from various statements of different people, witnesses to weepings; but even the marvelous may become familiar, and worse, dull, after many presentations.

As another backup sign, or signs, a Head of Christ in Agony (a copy of the Olimpias one), owned by the lady, wept tears in the spring of 1973 at her home. It also shed blood on Good Friday, 1973 and Good Friday, 1974. Here is a quote from a sworn affidavit:

"In early April, 1973, I saw tears coming down from the face of the Head of Christ in Agony that Mrs. X owns. On Good Friday of 1973 I saw blood running from the face of the same Head of Christ. I was asked to taste it and it did taste like blood. A little blood came from the crown of thorns area after a lot came from the eyes and mouth." — that from a young man who has since served in one of our Armed Forces and is presently studying for the priesthood in Rome.

We resist giving further accounts of the many weepings of the lady's Fatima statue, or other wonders connected with this lady. We skip many things of interest to concentrate on objective tears. The lady is merely an "instrument" as she has frequently pointed out. The thing to do, she says, is to act on the tears and the message. Perhaps many a reader has got the message already, but we will say a little about it in our concluding chapter, even a little in this one.

It should be apparent that these weepings are obviously not frauds. Let anybody try to prove such allegations before a civil or ecclesiastical court. Shall we attribute the weepings to the devil and contend that God permits the most sacred images to be used by the demon? And when all kinds of spiritual and moral good have come about for many witnessing or hearing of the weepings? The devil is not allowed to work a genuine sign or miracle. If we eliminate the demon, where do we end then? If we attribute such marvels to the demon then how can we judge any miracle of God as genuine?

Child witnesses have simply said, "Mary is crying!" Intelligent adults, but with the simplicity of faith have said, "Mary weeps!" and "Our Lord wept!" The demon does not move hearts through holy tears. But Christ and Mary do.

In brief the lady of the weeping Fatima statues would sum up the Blessed Virgin's substantial message thus: "Stop sinning! Return to my Son. Go to your Eucharistic Lord with hearts in adoration, reparation and please for His Merciful Love. Or face great tribulations!"

(According to our best information, the original International Fatima Pilgrim Virgin statue that wept so much in the United States, and especially at New Orleans, Atlanta and in New York in 1972, and which statue has been in Brazil and South America, returned officially to the United States about late summer of 1982, after an interim of eight years. It has begun to tour the United States again.)

> "If the Church has accepted the Message of Fatima, it is above all because that message contains a truth and a call whose basic content is the truth and the call of the Gospel itself."
>
> — John Paul II, homily at Fatima.

North American Pilgrim Virgin weeping June 14, 1972

XIII — THE LOUISIANA SEQUENCES OF WEEPING FATIMA STATUES

"Through her tears she looked up to heaven." **Dn. 13:35.**

In this chapter our subject embraces the weeping Fatima statues of a gentleman who is an exile from Communist Cuba (as the lady in the previous chapter is an exile from Communist Poland). Some readers will recognize him. We shall designate him as "CE". When in this chapter we mention Fatima statues weeping in Louisiana, let it be clear, we are not referring here to the North American International Fatima Pilgrim Virgin statue, associated with the lady "AW" treated of in the preceding chapter, which wept twice at New Orleans in July 1972.

Nor are we referring at all to the lady's own Fatima statue which wept so many times and in so many cities of the United States as has already been seen (and has been weeping again, recently, in 1981, at this writing), although that Fatima statue was with the lady at many talks in Louisiana in late 1972 and in 1974. I am not aware of the latter Fatima statue ever weeping in Louisiana although other wonders (credible) have been claimed in its presence. Nor am I referring to at least two to four other Fatima statues claimed as having wept elsewhere in Louisiana.

About 1950-1951, the International North American Fatima Pilgrim Virgin statue referred to above, then on its early tours, was passing through Havana, Cuba. Its route was not planned to pass by the home of a certain small boy who was suffering from asthma and also running a high fever. But due to unforeseen and apparently highly providential circumstances a traffic diversion, due to a vehicle accident that harmed no one, caused the statue to be rerouted nearby.

The four-year old's maternal grandmother, a pious woman full of faith (who ended up in a Castro concentration camp and was not allowed to be released to her family in her old age and died there), grabbed the child and threw her shawl around it. His mother protested he would die, but the grandmother ran down the street where the Virgin's statue was passing by.

The grandmother lifted him up to the famous image of Our Lady of Fatima, and the boy, now a man, clearly remembers the incident. Although his uncle, a doctor had scheduled him to go into the hospital the next day, the boy, after being presented to Our Lady of Fatima, returned home to eat a hearty meal. He was well and the hospital trip was cancelled.

Years later, this boy, an exile in the United States from Castro's Communistic Cuba, came to New Orleans. There, become a grown man, he acquired from Fatima, a large beautiful Our Lady of Fatima statue of his own. This statue was to shed tears many times in the metropolitan area of New Orleans.

Why New Orleans again, some may ask? That is part of the puzzle-picture, if there really is one. Why did the North American International Pilgrim Virgin statue, which wept in so many places, have its most famous weeping in New Orleans? Why was another famous Fatima statue ("AW's"), which wept in many places in the United States, also present several times in New Orleans? And, why, only recently, 1980, did another Fatima statue weeping sequence occur in the metropolitan New Orleans area?

A number of things seem to be going together—Italy with a number of weepings in 1972 alone; New Orleans, Atlanta, New York, Washington, (U.S. capital!), all with famous weepings that involved two famous Fatima statues in 1972! And now the New Orleans, Louisiana area would experience two sequences of Fatima statues (from Fatima) in a good number of weepings, 1975 and 1980. It is something to think about; Italy, the home of Catholicism, and the United States of America, the one great political and military opponent to Communistic Russia.

Further, the two "seers" or instruments, are both exiles from *Communistic* dominated countries, *Poland* in the Russian orbit, and *Cuba* on the perimeter of America's southern shores. And the common link in both areas of extraordinary weepings is a number of FATIMA statues, Fatima statues that remind us of the *Fatima message* and *prophecies*, especially of the ever increasing power and spread of atheistic, Communistic Russia with its persecutions; and the danger and ultimate threat of nuclear war.

Of further interest: The International North American Pilgrim Fatima statue before which the Cuban exile was cured as a boy in Havana, wept in the presence of the Polish exile lady in New Orleans, 1972. Then a few years later the Cuban exile's own Fatima statue would be weeping in New Orleans.

Pardon the digression. But the message is very urgent to save what yet can be saved, and, as the Bible says "to strengthen what remains." And to put things together!

The exiled Cuban, near thirty years of age and a father of small boys, one day, 1975, was in his home in metropolitan New Orleans, when something happened to tremendously alter his life and that of many others. The beautiful Fatima statue he had received from Fatima was in his bedroom, and all things normal. Yes, the statue had been blessed by the Bishop of Leiria (the diocese where Fatima is) and placed by the tombs of the saintly Jacinta and Francesco, who were the chosen children of the Fatima apparitions, along with still living Sister Lucia.

In June 1975 (three years after the New Orleans Pilgrim Virgin weepings of 1972 and after two speaking tours of the lady with her own Fatima statue in the southern Louisiana area, Dec. 1972 and Oct. 1974). the feasts of the Sacred Heart of Jesus and the Immaculate Heart of Mary (no accident for the liturgical timing!) came together. The Fatima statue of the Cuban exile began to weep on Thursday afternoon, June 5th, and wept at certain times through the Feast of the Sacred Heart of Jesus, Friday, June 6, and that of the Immaculate Heart of Mary, June 7, 1975. It came about like this.

A small son of the owner of the statue ran into the kitchen shouting, "Our Lady is crying!" The father told his little son, "I don't want you to tell lies," and he threatened to spank him.

"You can spank me if you want to," his son replied, "but Our Lady *IS* crying!" The father hurried into the bedroom. His Fatima statue *was* crying. A number of witnesses were called in, even with time for some of them to arrive some distance through phone calls. These first tears lasted from 2:30 p.m. to 3:15 p.m., that Thursday, June 5, 1975. The statue wept again that Thursday in the late evening before the morrow's feast of the Sacred Heart of Jesus. Then began a series or sequence of weepings.

In the early morning hours, about three a.m., Friday, June 6, 1975, the Fatima statue wept again — by then the feast of the Sacred Heart of Jesus. Later in the early morning of the feast there were messages claimed from Mary, and another weeping. Mary asked for a vigil to be kept through all that night Friday until the feast of Her Immaculate Heart, Saturday, June 7th.

The statue shed tears seven times from Thursday, June 5th to Friday, June 6th. At times when certain persons were leaving the home they would be called back or return to witness more crying. On, Saturday, June 7th, around 5:30 a.m., early morning of the feast of the Immaculate Heart of Mary, Our Lady of Fatima, who had asked, there at Fatima, for a vital devotion to Her Immaculate Heart and for the consecration of Russia, by the Pope and all the bishops of the world, to Her Immaculate Heart, wept through her statue for a long period.

Any reasonable person can see and understand that with so many weepings, and a good number of witnesses still available, the Church at any time can secure any number of statements or affidavits regarding the various weepings. It is materially and legally impossible to deny all these weepings. Besides, there were some photos taken, and cameras neither suffer from mass hysteria, neuroses nor hypnotism. But these first weepings were, tremendous as the impact on the witnesses, just the beginning.

Let us cull from a few statements of witnesses.

"I myself have witnessed this same above mentioned statue of Our Lady of Fatima weep at least twenty (20) times . . . I tasted the tears twice and both times the tears were salty."

Another witness saw the statue cry fifteen times. One lady who witnessed about twelve weepings, said of the very first: "We found X embracing his two small sons, and all three were crying very hard, watching and weeping for 'Our Lady's sadness'."

Of a later June 8, 1975 weeping of the statue, a man said: "I, not only saw the statue of Our Lady of Fatima weep, but touched her left eyeball with the little finger of my left hand. To my amazement, the eye felt human—actually moved at the touch of my finger, which became wet with a tear. I then tasted the tear which was salty. After She stopped crying I touched the eye again and it was hard. This incident impressed me so deeply that I have begun praying more."

Of a Wednesday, July 9, 1975 weeping an adult woman witnessed: ". . . Our Lady weeping! She looked so sad and pitiful — the handkerchief that had been placed on her hands was actually soaked and dripping. I was so moved to see this pitiful sight I shed tears myself." — *That, weeping* with Mary, and *prayer*, as above, seem part of getting, and of catching on to the message!

The above owner of the New Orleans weeping Fatima statue claims a mission from Mary to fight Communism with Mary's own "weapons" (as She reportedly called them): reparation, adoration of the Most Blessed Sacrament, the praying of her holy rosary. The "seer" claims he was told that time is short.

At his home, (a second one, removed from the original house of weepings, but where there have been other weepings), his first Fatima statue is enshrined back of a lovely altar in a beautiful chapel. People are allowed to have prayer meetings and devotions there. The statue is called the "stationery" Virgin because it remains enshrined there. The owner estimates it has wept fifty-three (53) times. (Yes, the number of weepings is similar to that of the lady's own Fatima statue of the previous chapter.)

I said, "first" Fatima statue. This man is associated with other statues or images that have wept: A Head of Christ in Agony, a Sacred Heart of Jesus statue, the Corpus of a crucifix, an Immaculate Conception statue, and a second Fatima statue, all kept in his home, although occasionally one or two have gone out on pilgrimage.

Ironically enough, his first Fatima statue. of cedarwood, which came from Fatima itself, arrived on a Communist ship in New Orleans, Dec. 8, (feast of the Immaculate Conception) 1974. (The lady from Poland was with her own weeping Fatima statue in New Orleans a little earlier in October, 1974). Several weepings of the above images of the Cuban exile have involved blood, as from the Head of Christ in Agony.

In the fall of 1976 our Cuban exile went to New York City to bring home to New Orleans his second Fatima statue as it came from Portugal. One of the pilots on the return trip had lived in Portugal. This pilot happily laid the large cedarwood statue, with great care across four empty plane seats. In the air this Fatima statue wept on the trip South. One lady who witnessed it, on arriving in New Orleans, returned to the Sacraments after a several years absence.

This large, beautiful Fatima statue, (referred to as "The Pilgrim" because it is taken from the house to circulate) with a lovely mantle (added) wept, on the owner's estimate, since in his possession, about twenty times, up to and including a special sequence of weepings in 1980. There is hardly any point in detailing all its weepings. The Church does not want her priests to say multiple Masses in one day, normally, because, for one reason, even a priest can get too used to the sacred and sublime.

When one sees a weeping or weepings of a statue or hears of them very often, one can become emotionally immune to even Mary crying through her images, or Christ "vicariously" bleeding from an image of His Head in Agony. This author recalls, from his own experiences, that a first witnessed crying is very awe inspiring or impressive. But one can get used to miracles in time, and to weepings. But many different individuals benefit from the many different weepings, at least at times. Some persons never believe; some — even as with Christ — reject great spiritual favors or graces.

It should be pointed out that, again, at the conjunction of the feasts of the Sacred Heart of Jesus and the Immaculate Heart of Mary, in 1980, the second "big" Fatima statue of the gentleman above, "The Pilgrim", wept again.

This was the fifth anniversary of the original 1975 weepings of the "stationary" Fatima statue. Over these two feasts and beyond in June 1980, the "Pilgrim" wept several times on the first day, June 5, 1980, the first weeping "heavily", for about an hour and a half. It also wept on June 6th, June 7th and June 8th, 1980.

The second weeping of the first day, June 5, 1980, (of this new sequence of Fatima statue weepings near New Orleans) lasted from about 20 minutes to half an hour. The third weeping that day occurred downstairs when the "Pilgrim" had been brought downstairs (it is usually kept upstairs in the gentleman's bedroom), and placed on the round table in the living-room quarters off the kitchen.

The fourth weeping that day was from about 7:00 p.m. to 8:30 p.m. It was weeping during a Holy Hour with people still at prayer in the chapel. People participating in the Holy Hour ran out of cloths to absorb the tears; and the cloths were soaking wet. People were asking, "Have we not done enough, is there not enough reparation, Blessed Mother?"

The Fatima statue kept weeping. Over the next three days it wept. About a dozen times was the final total.

Of the first of those weepings, a lady testified: "I took pictures of Our Lady of Fatima statue . . . and this statue began to weep. As I tasted the tears, they were salty to the taste. As I took more pictures of the statue, I noticed through the lens, that the pupils of the statue's eyes were dilating.

"This was witnessed by A, B and C. Being Our Lady's 'feast' of Her Tears ((5th anniversary of 1975 weeping)), others at the chapel that day also witnessed the Madonna weeping."

An incident that day, typical of what has happened at a number of weepings of holy images in the United States follows. Present before the third weeping that June 5, 1980, of the large "Pilgrim" Fatima statue, was a man who doubted the authenticity of the claimed statue weepings. He was a member of a certain group and away from the Church. This incredulous man had spoken of a probable tubing placed in the statue to "pipe" "tears" to the eyes.

The Fatima "Pilgrim" statue was to be placed downstairs. The owner, the incredulous man mentioned above, and another gentleman carried the rather heavy image downstairs. As they came down the stairs the statue began to weep.

Seeing the statue weeping while in motion, the "unbeliever" fell on his knees and began crying himself. He returned to the Church. This author could relate similar "confrontations" by the Fatima statue of the lady written about in the previous chapter, when Mary also took up challenges by skeptics and through her Fatima statues wept in their presence.

The weepings of the various images of "CE" have been confined, except for the plane in transit weeping, as far as this author is aware, to the metropolitan New Orleans area. Most weepings have occurred in the first or second home, some outside, as in a procession or prayer gathering, and some when a statue was in circulation; one crucifix, apparently when it was at a Catholic institution. Another crucifix at the gentleman's home. Regarding blood tears or weeping we should mention in particular a Head of Christ in Agony.

But why detail all weepings? It should suffice to say several individual sacred images in the Cuban exile's home have wept on various occasions. (As we have seen, several images connected with the lady in the previous chapter have wept; a number of images of the deceased Teresa Musco wept.) But the main, long and "big" weepings have been of *Fatima* statues. The fundamental and overall message of tears is from statues of Our Lady of *Fatima.* It was so with the Polish lady, long *Fatima* statue weepings. Always there is enunciated a fundamental Fatima message of reparation, prayer, Eucharistic adoration, Mount Carmel scapular, daily rosary, etc.

It is interesting that at the first weeping of the first Fatima statue of the Cuban exile, one of the initial witnesses, a gentleman opened a Jerusalem Bible at random and his finger fell on the passage, "the cry of anguish in great distress". The same gentleman (who witnessed many weepings), when he asked school children, "Why do you think statues weep?", happened to open the Bible then, and it was at the heading, "Jesus weeps over Jerusalem."

A laboratory analysis showed liquid from one of the above Fatima statues, the "Stationery One" to be that of human-tear content, for instance, sodium, potassium and chloride elements (July 8, 1975 Pathology Laboratory report).

A final "Cuban" note. When Castro's Cuban Government would not permit the entry of the National Fatima Pilgrim Virgin statue intended for Cuba, it was decided to place it in the Church titled Our Lady of Fatima in Florida nearest to Cuba. The statue found at Inverness, Florida an honored home where Father James Cottrell developed a wonderful Marian shrine. The shrine, with its nocturnal adoration, vigils, Fatima Rosary, and Eucharistic devotions, a flourishing place of Catholic piety, was also the site of the first three-day cenacle of Father Gobbi's Marian Movement of Priests in America, 1978 — a great compliment to the pastor. The Cuban exile once was present at the Inverness shrine with his Fatima statue in an impressive procession. In the past thousands of good laity and many excellent priests from wide areas found much inspiration at the Inverness Our Lady of Fatima church shrine.

In the yard of the same Cuban exile there is an outdoor shrine to Our Lady of Fatima, all beautifully and tastefully arranged. In early

February, 1982, the large marble statue of Our Lady of Fatima there wept for about forty-five minutes. It was around the feast of the Presentation of the Lord. It was mainly from the left eye, down to the nose, etc. The Cuban gentleman commented that it is something to see a wood-carved or painted statue of Mary weep. But when one sees Our Lady of Fatima shaped in marble weeping it adds a new dimension to the reaction of the viewer. Indeed, "the very stones cry out!" As Our Lord said before His Passion, if you silence the voices of the children — "prophets" — the very stones will cry out.

In an appendix we tell of the reported apparitions of Mary in Cuba, off Havana, over the bay waters. In brief the Communist authorities are alarmed and handicap the Cuban "pilgrims". One of the recently reported communications from Our Lady reputedly amounts to this: "If you bring Me back to Cuba I will give Cuba back to you!"

In this connection, the gentleman who has been subject of this chapter, the Cuban exile has just published at this revised writing a book, *Nuestra Señora De La Caridad Del Cobre, Our Lady of Charity, Patroness of Cuba.* It is in English and Spanish and gives the history of the devotion to Our Lady of Charity of Cobre, the Patroness of Cuba, novena prayers, etc. As a foreword of the gentleman says: "Let us be mindful that the Island of Cuba, only 90 miles from this great country, is a threat to peace here in America, as well as in this hemisphere. Let us all pray to Our Lady of Charity, Patroness of Cuba, that the Communist forces be dissolved and that Cuba may regain its freedom, so that it can live in harmony once again with the American people, who have done so much for the Cubans in exile." — Thinking persons will see, many things hang together!

> "No matter how formidably communism bristles with tanks and rockets . . . it is doomed never to vanquish Christianity." — Alexander Solzhenitsyn, London, May 10, 1983.

XIV — WEEPING IMAGES OF CHRIST

***"I water you with tears."* Is. 16:9.**

We have entitled this book, *THE TEARS OF MARY — AND FATIMA*. WHY? with Mary accented because many more tears are reported of Mary and her images than of her Divine Son and His. This is natural because a woman, and especially a mother of many children weeps more than a man.

The other apparent reason, if we can venture an opinion, is that God has given Mary a very special mission in our times (as Mary plainly states in Father Gobbi's book) as is apparent from her many apparitions in our times and her numerous statues vicariously weeping for her. This is also obvious, it would seem, from the importance of her great mission announced at Fatima, a mission which will go on continuously until the era of peace, destined for the Church and the world, as promised by Mary and through her Immaculate Heart, will come about.

There is a reference to the Child of the Mother in Franciscan history where the Divine Child *wept*. In the *Franciscan Book of Saints* we read of Blessed John Lobedau, born at Thorn in West Prussia, who became an early celebrated Franciscan preacher in that area of recent conversion to Christianity. The Blessed Mother "frequently appeared to him with her Divine Child, and conversed with him . . ."

Father John was once living in the convent of the Franciscans at Kulmsee, when certain of his brethren passing by his cell were amazed to hear the voice of a woman coming from within it. They were suspicious, because he had been considered a saint. More, presently they heard the voice of a child's crying.

Receiving no answer to their raps on his cell door, they threw it open, only to find John alone, absorbed in prayer and weeping very much. The Superior, who was called the Father Guardian, ordered John under obedience to divulge what had taken place.

John told them that the Blessed Mother along with her Child Jesus had been in the cell with him. The reason why the Child Jesus had wept was that the Child knew that the Catholic Religion, only recently introduced in the area, was soon to be exterminated and the places of Catholic worship destroyed.

Yes, Our Lord, too, has had his apparitions, and some weeping images also, even to blood.

We are not going into apparitions here except perhaps with a passing remark. In going back to the weeping images in Italy we might recall

My wounds, but to My Mother, I gave My perfect likeness in her interior, after My Passion, with all My sufferings, My wounds and the pains My Heart underwent." — *Diary*.

Christ, speaking of His Mother's later life solitude, said: "Her title of Mother of all mankind, Mary won by the martyrdom of her solitude after My death. Has the world been aware of this? Does it appreciate it and is it grateful for it? The time has come when the children should show that they are real children, showing their veneration for this heart broken by this subtle and most painful martyrdom, lived through for the sake of their own happiness. There Mary gained graces for each and every man. It is time for her to be thanked." — *Diary*, June 30, 1917.

> "Woman, why are you weeping? Who is it you are looking for?" — John 20:15

Some recently learned information might be appended here. A recently arriving American "seer", a young mother with children, claims a vision of Christ in the Garden of Gethsemane, bleeding all over His Body. She also states that the Lord is saddened because certain natural disasters, "small signs" sent by God, are explained away and credit is not given where it is due.

This young mother also claims messages or locutions concerning an increased activity or outpouring of the Holy Spirit, a major war, the "chastisement", a great "darkness", fire from the heavens seeking out the incorrigibly wicked, and God promising protection for His own. She affirms the authenticity of the Garabandal "Warning" and "Miracle" prophecies. When about a dozen priests together interviewed this young woman they seemed convinced of her own authenticity.

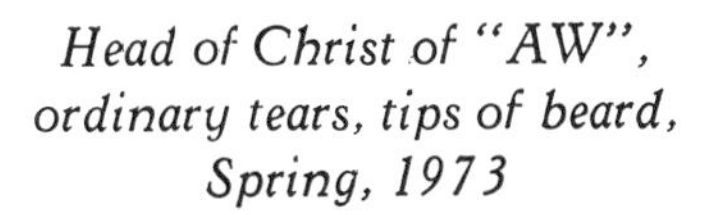

Head of Christ of "AW", ordinary tears, tips of beard, Spring, 1973

XV — WHY LOUISIANA?

"Those that sow in tears shall reap rejoicing." **Ps. 126:5**

If we consider the above question from the practical viewpoint of a former soldier and member of the Eighth Air Force, the author, southern Louisiana holds several prime war-targets. Many Americans do not realize that New Orleans in many respects is the No. 1 port in the United States. It also controls the Mississippi River valley.

With its oil and gas resources and its petro-chemical plants strung in great numbers from New Orleans to Baton Rouge, flanking the Mississippi River on both banks, and others over to Lake Charles near the Texas border, beside the Louisiana Super-port offshore in the Gulf, a forest of oil rigs and explorations in the same Gulf, and underground oil-storage reserves — the whole area is simply a super-target for Soviet Russia.

Russia does not have to fire long-range intercontinental ballistic missiles from U.S.S.R. territory either. A single Russian submarine in the Gulf or Atlantic could do untold nuclear destruction in southern Louisiana. Further, nearby Cuba is a Communist haven and has betrayed the Americas in linking up with the Russian Communist atheistic Government.

We saw the Cuban exile's sensible words about Communist Cuba's nearby threat to America, in his foreword to his book, *Our Lady of Charity, Patroness of Cuba (La Virgen de la Caridad).* Again we see how many things go together. Is not nuclear destruction for the United States, and here, especially southern Louisiana, a probability in our times, when the nuclear scientists themselves have often placed the hands of their nuclear war-clock at a few minutes before midnight?

During World War II, Louisianians could go down to the Gulf coast areas of the state and see the oil tankers blazing after Nazi submarine hits. That was peanuts then! Children's firecrackers! Tomorrow they might see a good part of southern Louisiana ablaze — or annihilated!

Besides the dangers from non-natural disaster elements, Mary has also warned us against natural calamities, which could include, for Louisiana, recurrent river-floods and hurricanes. With the wrong combination of wind and water a good portion of the New Orleans population could be decimated.

Another factor for Louisiana could be the possible hope-for strengthening of the people spiritually and with that the deterrence of or lessening of the varied possible disasters, because of a hearty response with prayer, penance, reparation, Eucharistic adoration, etc.

We might note another mark of supernatural activities in the way Mary, like Christ, does things. Mary chooses out of the way places and little, humble people for her visitations. So, in 1858 she chose Bernadette and a drab rural area at remote Massabielle of Lourdes. So, in 1917 Mary chose the little, hidden mountainous hamlet of Fatima with its ignorant little shepherds as her chosen instruments for world-shaking announcements.

Remember, Christ chose a shepherdess, Joan of Arc, from little Domremy, a teenager, *La Pucelle,* "The Maid", to lead the armies of France. Christ and Mary love to confound the ordinary ways and wisdom of men. "My ways are not your ways," says the Lord. So, perhaps with Louisiana!

We find chosen instruments, like the Polish lady and the Cuban man in the United States with weeping Fatima statues, who, like Father Gobbi ask, "Why me?" The reply is simply this: It is the work of God that is going to be done, not that of the instruments in God's or Mary's hands.

Louisiana has been regarded by many as poor and backward, with much illiteracy, and with many unfair declarations made about the State. Louisiana has its faults and it may be due some punishments or chastisements for its good. But I never heard that the Sacrament of Penance or Reconciliation was instituted for only particular areas of the world. New Orleans, true, is a pleasure-loving city, but a lot of its festivals, Mardi Gras, parades, Sugar and Super Bowls, restaurants, hotels, etc., are for the tourists trade and business reasons also.

There is the sorrier side of part of the *Vieux Carré* or French Quarter and much crime. As in Paris saints and sinners can live side by side. Yet, it is hard to see that New Orleans in itself is any worse than any number of other large American cities, or those of other countries. New Orleans has many virtues, much hospitality and many charities.

Be that as it may, this author is aware of a sort of cartoon-picture revelation, private, through a chosen little seer some years ago, far away in Sicily. Of New Orleans was depicted in brief: "New Orleans — My scandal", with a cross drawn in each of the four corners. The reasons why a "scandal" (and perhaps moreso then, some years ago? — or less?) were not given.

Perhaps mainly because Christ and Mary often choose a humble, remote place, not the Londons or New Yorks — big cities — nor a Paris of the world, perhaps that is the reason there has been so much image-weeping activity in southern Louisiana in recent years. Perhaps a message is still coming out (in 1972, remember, from New Orleans a message was intended for the whole world, but only the picture of the tears got out, not the message) from a place lowly in the eyes of the world. "What good can come out of Nazareth?"

However, there were real tears shed in Louisiana and a message meant to help the world, and in particular the United States. And down there the tears have continued to flow, and very recently. Tears from 1972 to 1982! Perhaps some persons will begin to catch on to their message?

Again, Christ and Mary seem to be working these days through the few rather than the many, since so little publicity has been given these unusual happenings in Louisiana. But then, many Catholics have never heard of Fatima, and very little about the Blessed Mother Herself!

Perhaps, too, from another spiritual viewpoint, this is a special grace for the people of this Louisiana area for the present and the future. Who can tell how things will go, how war, conquest or other disastrous events will affect any particular part of the world? Reportedly, years ago, the Bavarian stigmatist, Teresa Neumann of Konnersreuth, forecast that the United States would suffer from natural disasters, but reportedly also that there was a special part of the United States where it would be favored because of the devotion there of the people to the holy rosary.

Mr. Alfred Williams, the custodian of the National Pilgrim Virgin Fatima statue for the United States, who has traveled endlessly around the country with it, has been of the opinion that an unusual rosary-saying belt devoted to Mary begins in southern Louisiana, and extends westward. Moving through the Southwest this is augmented by notable daily Mass attendance. (He said this very recently.) At any rate, Mary's many vicarious weepings in Louisiana may express her merciful love, a mother desiring to warn, to protect, and to inspire a gigantic reparation effort to save others. Remember, Eucharistic devotion and rosary recitation were among the requests of the lady with the weeping Fatima statue.

Be that as it may, we have at present, under testing, other claims of Marian manifestations in southern Louisiana, down a bayou toward the Gulf of Mexico. A gentleman there claims that the Blessed Mother wants a shrine to be built in that area because "there will be many sick". Sick people, it is said, will be cured there. Again, this may be a part of filling in the larger picture. There are some unusual angles to this claim that involve other interesting people but we cannot go into that here. We are merely reporting a happening that we believe should call for an awaiting of more developments.

The Fatima message here too is central. The usual things, prayer, reparation, rosary, devotion to Our Lord in the Blessed Sacrament, are asked. Many people seem to be led to more devout lives. Cures and spiritual favors have been reported. Just the other day an older, balanced priest told this author of his having brought two persons from a distant state who were cured. As usual there has been some confusion and controversy.

The man has been obedient to his Bishop. The matter at present seems to depend upon certain developments or further signs that would endorse the "prophetic" declaration. This author is not pronouncing on anything, but he is aware of many spiritual "good fruits" proceeding from this "mission" and good priests and people who believe it substantially authentic. Only time will bring further light.

So, all these things may go together in a larger pattern, either for close-by activity or far-reaching effects; for admonishment, but also for encouragement, and even reward. We can only say, like the song, Let the love of God and fellow man, and peace begin with me! Let reparation begin with me! And let nuclear warheads and missiles be far from us all! Reparation, from whatever humble or remote place it has as its inspiration and start, can spread all over, and save much if not all the world from great tribulations and disasters.

The overall message again is that Our Lady is weeping through her Fatima images again and again. A Fatima image can only recall Fatima itself, the apparitions there, the urgent requests made by the Mother of God, Our Lady of Fatima, her prophecies and her promises. And simple requests like prayers and penance, like rosary recitation and scapular devotion, like genuine renewal and a return to her Eucharistic Son.

The matter is urgent! The world sits, or rather, sleeps atop neutron bombs and nuclear warheads. When this author was stationed on the American airbase at Cheddington, England, one could watch, as dusk approached, seemingly endless RAF bombers heading for the Continent. They could number 500. One could only pray for the thousands in enemy territory who would soon be dead as the air raid sirens wailed and the radios cried, "Achtung — Luftwaffe!" — "Enemy aircraft approaching!"

In the early morning one could watch the Flying Fortresses and Liberators of the American Eighth Air Force gathering in the blue skies for a big daylight raid, again as many as 500 bombers. As we observed before, it was all "firecrackers" compared to the destructive power of one modern American submarine equipped with nuclear warheads. And there would be practically no warning time! When shall the world heed the plea: "Return to my Son!" When shall it take the only true remedies against utter destruction! When help Mary to "Bring my children back to God."

"Blessed are they that mourn, for they shall be comforted."—
Mt. 5:5

XVI — ABOUT ITALY AND AMERICA

"Bitterly she weeps at night, tears upon her cheeks." **Lam. 1:2.**

How does one react to much evidence, many photos of one's Blessed Mother and one's Saviour in the shedding of numerous tears, even the agony depicted by streaming tears of blood? In a way, is this perhaps more striking, the latter, than recalling the Garden of Gethsemane Sweat? We have no pictures of that.

We do have many *apparitions* of Jesus and Mary streaming with blood. We also have many *images* of them shedding normal human tears copiously, or streaming with shocking tears of blood — even blood-tears falling over a globe of the earth held in Mary's hands. Even from Bambinos!

What was — and is! — the great significance of so many remarkable weepings as we have seen, that occurred in 1972? We have indicated a bit the possible reason, that the year 1972 offered the last chances to make universal reparation for the world's sins before a judgment was made. It appears the judgment-sentence made then, or the permitting of many tribulations to come, has been unfolding since then, and continues to do so. This does not mean that many local areas of trial cannot be helped, nor the general purification lessened or shortened, nor preliminary tribulations not be modified.

But there does appear to be a moral certainty now that all the prophecies of Fatima will be fulfilled, and that the Third Secret will continue on in its unfolding course translating into action. And it seems events forecast in the Twelfth Chapter of *Apocalypse* or the *Book of Revelation* can well be in motion now, as it is allegedly claimed by Mary, through a favorite priest seer, at least in some aspects or stages.

Again, we must remember, time and action as seen by God, and events on the other side, are not according to our measurements. For instance the word "soon" in prophetic announcements is often "jumped" by seers themselves and by interpreters. So we must not try to sharpen focuses too closely or "Zoom" in on forecasted events. In a word, we should avoid fitting in supernatural sequences on a human calendar.

But, why so many weeping images centered about Italy and the United States, and more locally so in America, about southern Louisiana? Italy, almost renegade in the practice of the Catholic Faith for millions of its children, a once glorious daughter of the Church, the land area of the Spouse of Christ the Church, is given over, in many of her so-called Catholic children, to the harlotry of much immorality and association with atheistic Communism. For Italy, and for the Church housed there, the warnings seem clear enough as do the messages. Perhaps a few further prophecies of Sister Elena Aiello, concerning Italy will be helpful if also disturbing.

In the Second-Third Quarters, 1981 issue of *Divine Love* magazine, further previously unpublished prophecies of Sister Elena Aiello were published. They, in part, mention Italy and Rome in a manner more explicit for forewarnings than we have heard of as yet:

On Good Friday, March 23, 1951, the Madonna said: "All the world will soon be at war, and the streets will be stained with blood . . . All nations will be punished, because sin has spread all over the world . . . My heart bleeds for Italy also, which will be safe only in part for the Pope!"

On December 8, 1956, feast of the Immaculate Conception, Mary said: "Italy, my daughter, will be humiliated, purified in blood, and must suffer much, because many are the sins of this beloved country, seat of the Vicar of Christ . . . There will be a great revolution and streets will be red with blood."

In 1959, after Jesus, dripping with blood, appeared to Sister Elena, Mary appeared, sad and shedding tears, and, among other prophecies such as foretelling a purifying fire to fall from heaven, concerning Italy said: "Russia will march upon all the nations of Europe, particularly Italy, and will raise her flag over the dome of St. Peter's. Italy will be severely tried by a great revolution, and Rome will be purified in blood for its many sins, especially those of impurity! The flock is about to be dispersed and the Pope must suffer greatly!"

Mary foretells a great purifying fire to fall on the earth in general, but through Her intercession Italy will be spared so that: "I will manifest my partiality for Italy, which will be preserved from the fire, but the skies will be covered with dense darkness, and the earth will be shaken by fearful earthquakes which will open deep abysses. Provinces and cities will be destroyed and all will cry out that the end of the world has come!" (Very recently, May, 1983, another American "mystic" affirms prophetically the "darkness" referred to above, and also a fire seeking out the wicked.)

These prophecies should suffice for explaining Mary's frequent weepings in Italy. Way back, Good Friday, April 8, 1955, Mary appeared, majestic but lovely, with tears on her cheeks and told Sister Elena: "But men ignore all these warnings, and are unwilling to be convinced that my tears are plain signs to serve notice that tragic events are hanging over the world, and that the hours of great trials are at hand."

1955! Need one say anymore than consider all the incredible number of weepings since! Where then does the world, and in particular, Italy, stand today?

Why the United States? Already this nation has held a glorious place in history. It has been a refuge for all the good aspirations of mankind and has been a home for liberty-loving people from over the entire world. It still continues to be so, although many rights are trampled on. Liberty has been turned into permissiveness and immorality flourishes among many.

That nation, America, which should be the major political and spiritual bastion against atheistic Communism, is becoming more and more degenerate in many areas of its moral and spiritual life; abortion, sexual immorality of all kinds, Sodoms and Gomorrahs of homosexuals and lesbians, pre-marital sex (plain fornication), adultery, divorce, broken families, child abuse and pornography, political corruption, disregard of holy days, cursing, disobedience, drunkedness, drugs, murder, etc.

It would seem that Mary and Christ are calling America to reform, to renewal, reparation, holiness, at least to normally good lives; to the restoration of America to a true place of world leadership; and perhaps the political and military defeat of atheistic, Communistic Soviet Russia.

In general, one might hazard that the numerous weepings of Christ and Mary through their images are meant first to buttress the faithful and strengthen them in faith and virtue, to call particular souls and groups to generous prayer, to move them to penance and reparation so as to help save others; to inspire some clergy and laity to be martyrs and victim souls. And all this to save the world or a particular area of it from moral, religious and actual physical destruction.

The latter material destruction will be due to the disasters men, by their own evil lives and errors, bring upon themselves, such as persecution, revolutions, civil and even nuclear war. The horrors attendant upon nuclear, nerve-gas or biological warfare are simply unimaginable and make World Wars I and II look like some early tribal bow-and-arrow incursions. The Biblical lines may well be fulfilled: "With desolation is the world laid desolate!"

Concerning the *United States,* Sister Elena Aiello reportedly had a message on July 2, 1958, that because of all the evil in the world, Italy would be washed in her own blood, France covered with rubble and much of the United States in the hands of the Communists except one area devoted to the Rosary.

In this author's opinion this does not necessarily mean Russian Communist armies actually in America though that, too, could happen after a sudden Russian nuclear attack. Rather, it could mean much of the country under control of atheistic-type thought and morals, and irreligion. Theresa Neumann, as the author recalls, reputedly forecast many natural disasters for America, a good number of which certainly have occurred in the United States in recent decades and many in 1983. One only has to consult Federal Emergency Relief for recent disaster areas in innumerable U.S. counties.

Sister Elena, however, on the feast of the Immaculate Heart of Mary, August 22, 1960, reported the Madonna as saying: "If the people do not recognize in these scourges [of nature] the warnings of Divine Mercy, and do not return to God with truly Christian living, another terrible war will come from the East to the West. Russia with her secret armies will battle America; will overrun Europe. The River Rhine will be overflowing with corpses and blood . . ."

World War III is commonly talked about these days. And it would be exactly around the Rhine that many Allied troops would be in battle. And, for years since 1960, Russia has surely secretly fought the United States by means of armies not her own.

So, the tears in America are both a blessing and a warning, an appeal, and an additional reason for the incurring of just judgments and punishments because of the rejection of such unusual and additional graces. The good will be protected and strengthened even to the glory of martyrdom or great suffering where necessary.

The evil, if they do not repent, will end up in utter and eternal ruin. And, as promised in so many apparitions, the mercy of God will always be there and the motherly intercession of Mary. This assurance of mercy has been broadcast in our day by chosen souls like Sister Josefa Menendez, Sister Faustina, "Marguerite" and others.

There is no reason for anyone to fear or panic. There is plenty of reason to fear being very foolish in not facing the reality of the times, or to hide one's head ostrich-like in the sands while disaster approaches. He who remains with Christ, with Mary, with the angels and saints — "Saint Michael, protect us, defend us in the battle!" — with the Holy Father, will triumph with them.

The victory has been promised. It is simply a matter of passing through the rough period of trial and purification before entering upon the period of peace and happiness which will come with the ultimate victory. *Christus vincit, Christus regnat, Christus imperat!* "Christ conquers, Christ reigns, Christ rules over all!" As Our Blessed Mother said at Fatima, "In the end my Immaculate Heart will triumph." — No doubt about that!

Then we shall know, one might forecast safely, that Mary shall have been the great Mediatrix of Graces and Co-Redemptrix as proven by her activities in these times, when she shall have helped save the souls of many from the attacks of the Red Dragon and from all evil. By the power and the will of Christ!

If it is true, "The earth will reveal the blood upon her and no longer conceal her slain", it is also true, "They who sow in tears will reap in joy!"

Concerning America and what it might sow and what it might reap, and its great national responsibility, other private revelations have recently come to the attention of the author. We might well round out here the pleas and tears of Mary in general with some special ones of "Our Lady of America".

These pleas are reported by a Religious in the United States, Sister M., member of a one time cloistered group in an active order and lately in a new contemplative group. The supernatural experiences in her life began about 1938 with flights of the spirit, locutions, etc.

Mary presented herself to Sister M. as "Our Lady of America". Among other things Mary desired that her children in America would be dedicated to her purity, would be sanctified in family life and would lead the world to peace. Mary wanted pilgrimages made to her national Shrine of the Immaculate Conception at Washington, D.C., and to be honored there as "Our Lady of America, the Immaculate Virgin".

Mary further instructed the said Religious to have a medal of Our Lady of America struck with a special picture of Our Lady on one side and a Coat of Arms of the Christian Family on the other. Our concern here is to limit our quotations of Mary's communications through this Sister to references concerning Mary's maternal grief and tears.

"On September 27, 1956, Our Lady again appeared to me while I was at prayer. She held the world in her hands. From her eyes tears were flowing upon it, as though she longed to clease it from its guilt. It was then that I heard these words filled with sorrow and longing:

" 'Behold, O my children, the tears of your Mother! Shall I weep in vain? Assuage the sorrow of my Heart over the ingratitude of sinful men by the love and chasteness of your lives. Will you do this for me, beloved children, or will you allow your Mother to weep in vain? I come to you, O children of America, as a last resort. I plead with you to listen to my voice.' "

In 1957 and 1958 Our Lady often gave warnings through Sister M. Speaking of suffering, anguish and punishment to come, Our Lady spoke sadly but hopefully: "My daughter, will my children in America listen to my pleadings and console my Immaculate Heart? Will my loyal sons carry out my desires and thus help me bring the peace of Christ once again to mankind? Pray and do penance, my sweet child, that this may come to pass. Trust me and love me; I so desire it. Do not forget your poor Mother, who weeps over the loss of so many of her children."

On the eve of February 11, 1958, Mary said: "Beloved daughter, you wonder at the sword and the deep wound it has made in my Heart. It is the sword of grief plunged therein by my children who refuse to let me teach them the true way."

On December 20, 1959, Our Lady said: "O my child, tell your spiritual father that I come again to warn and plead. Oh, penance, penance! How little my children understand it! They give me many words, but sacrifice themselves they will not. It is not me they love but themselves. Oh, what blindness, sweet child, what blindness! How it pierces my Heart!

"See, I weep, but my children show me no compassion. They behold the sword in my Heart but will make no move to withdraw it. I give them love; they give me only ingratitude.

"Weep, then, dear child, weep with your Mother over the sins of men. Intercede with me before the throne of mercy, for sin is overwhelming the world and punishment is not far away."

Although not directly connected with "tears", because of the significance for the United States, associated with so many Fatima tears, we think a late message or two should be included here. So, on November 22, 1980

"Dear child, unless the United States accepts and carries out faithfully the mandate given to it by heaven to lead the world to peace, there will come upon it and all nations a great havoc of war and incredible suffering. If, however, the United States is faithful to this mandate from heaven and yet fails in the pursuit of peace because the rest of the world will not accept or cooperate then the United States will not be burdened with the punishment about to fall."

Sister M. was assured by Mary that Saint Michael and the angels would help the people. Finally, January 23, 1981, "the danger is imminent, there is no time to lose." And, "Get this message to them quickly as the time is shorter than ever."

In view of the whole world picture and the widespread appeals and tears of Mary, the above messages seem to speak very coherently and very urgently to the people of the United States. It is urgent for Catholics in particular to spend, even *expend* themselves spiritually for their motherland and their Holy Mother Church.

(We note that one time the late Archbishop Leibold of Cincinnati was a spiritual director of Sister M. And he encouraged the publishing of her messages.)

> "As he (Abraham) looked down toward Sodom and Gomorrah and the whole region of the Plain, he saw dense smoke rising like fumes from a furnace." — Gen. 19:28.

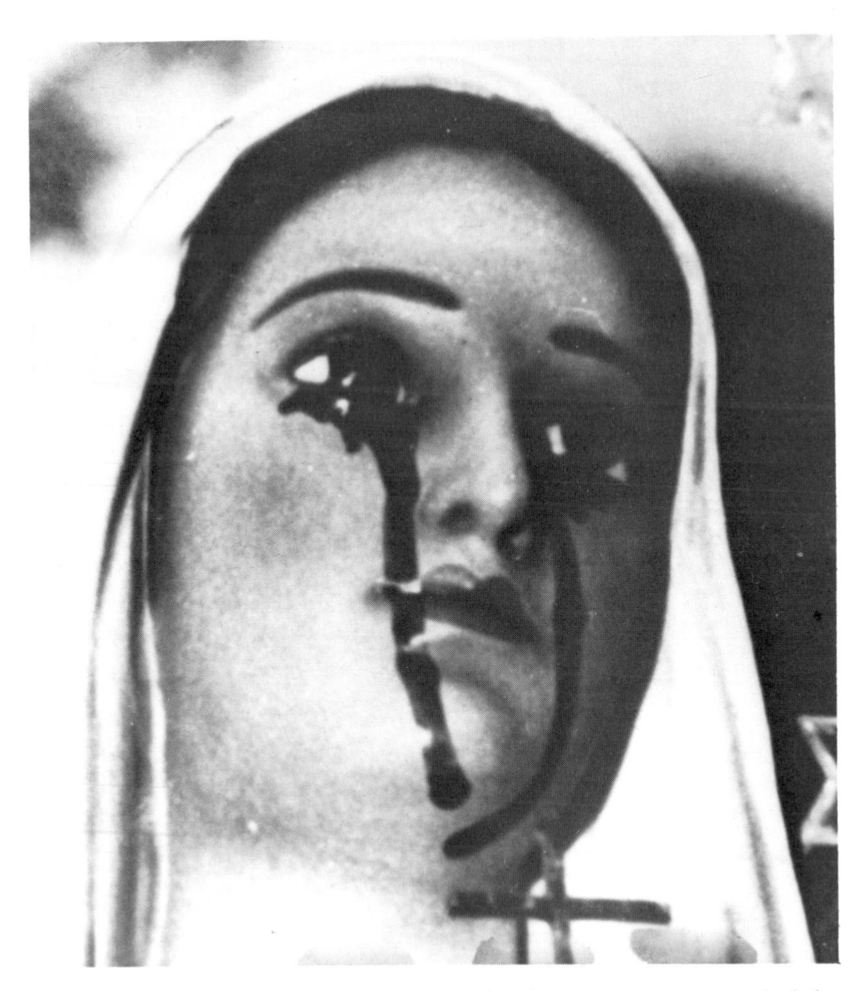

Regina Mundi, Queen of World, blood flowing over cross-topped globe, Porto San Stefano, Italy.

XVII — FIVE TYPES OF TEARS AND BLOOD

"I bear the brand marks of Jesus in my body." Gal. 6:17.

In this book we have concentrated mainly on tears of salt and tears of blood involving sacred images of Christ and Mary, and particularly — simply because of their prominence — involving images of Our Lady of Fatima. We have seen other kinds of tears and shedding of blood and perhaps we should recall them here briefly because they all go together, are inter-related and only when taken as a whole do they present the complete picture of the sorrowings, the tearful appeals and the warnings of Mary and her Divine Son.

— A —

First, we have heard of Christ and Mary appearing in great sadness and suffering, and at times shedding *ordinary tears or those of blood;* or even shedding blood as a stigmatist might do. There are a great number of such sorrowful appearances to saints, stigmatists and other chosen souls, especially to *victim* souls.

So, on a Saturday, February 25, 1922, Our Lord showed Himself to Sister Josefa Menendez clothed in sorrow over sins, crowned with thorns and His Holy Face streaming with blood. On February 28th Jesus said to her: "How great are the sins of men . . . but what distresses Me most is that they blindly fling themselves into hell . . . Do you understand My grief, Josefa? To see these souls that have cost Me My life, lost forever!"

As we have mentioned earlier, me do not weep as often as women. If it had been Mary in the last scene depicted she might have wept. With Our Lord in such appearances it is often a direct shedding of His Blood, patterned on His Passion and Crucifixion. The Gospel accounts do not say that Christ wept on the Cross. We do not know. But greater suffering, grief and sorrow were there than any tears could show.

So, too, Mary once said, 1959, to Sister Elena: "Oh, what a torture I feel in my heart . . . Italy shall be humiliated and purged in her blood." Some griefs are too deep for tears. Mary, however, did weep a number of times when appearing to Sister Elena Aiello.

The Madonna once appeared sad and shedding tears and said to Sister Elena: "This great mantle which you see is the expression of my mercy for covering sinners and saving them. Men, instead, cover themselves with even more filth, and do not want to confess their real faults. Therefore the justice of God will pass over the sinful World to purify humanity for so many sins, openly committed and hidden, especially those which corrupt youth."

We have seen other cases where chosen souls have witnessed the tears of Mary, including Berthe Petit, Marguerite, the Hungarian mother and the lady of the weeping Fatima statues in America. Remember, the latter said: "Some of you have seen the statue of Mary cry. I have seen Mary cry personally. It is not a pretty sight."

— B —

The second reference we had to tears and sorrow is where Mary or Christ, without weeping at the time of their apparitions, have *referred* to their tears or heartbreak. So we saw, in one case, in the book, *Our Lady Speaks to Her Beloved Priests,* where Mary speaks of her tears to Father Gobbi. Likewise She spoke to Sister Elena in 1955 (perhaps referring then to the great weepings at Syracuse in 1953). Also to the lady, "AW" in the United States in 1972 and to Mama Rosa in 1968. Also to others.

— C —

After recalling the apparitions of Christ and Mary we bring to mind a third kind of weeping of tears and shedding of blood, that of the stigmatists. We do so because the "framework" of these sufferings and manifestations of pain and grief come so close to those of Christ and Mary in their most touching, and we might say pitiful apparitions of tears and blood.

It is something to see an *image* of Christ or Mary cry, to gush salt-tears or shed those of blood. It is much more soul-shaking, arresting and impressive if we see fellow human beings not only shed normal tears of pain, but relive the passion and crucifixion of Christ in their bodies and right before our eyes.

Thus, one can see sanguinary photos of modern day victim souls while they went realistically, bloodily and dramtically through the Passion and Death of Christ, like a Theresa Neumann of Bavaria, a Sister Elena Aiello of Italy or a Rhoda Wise of Canton, Ohio. Even the pictures can make one shudder or avert one's eyes, to see a fellow human's eyes and face streaming with blood, and cloths and bed-clothes soaked in blood.

Some of these chosen victim souls are called to more regular and visible reparational sufferings conjoined with the Passion of Christ, as on every Friday. Others, while not so regularly or so periodically participating in the Passion of Our Lord (and the Sorrows of Mary) daily carry in themselves the stigmata, usually the five main wounds of Christ's side, hands and feet. They even walk with great pain (as Padre Pio could often be seen shuffling along and wincing with pain) or risk additional suffering as in their hands, by "official" examiners probing the wounds, or by thoughtless or over-enthusiastic, or merely curious and oafish persons grasping them.

(This author remembers, on a visit to Rhoda Wise years ago, how she told me that some thoughtless person when meeting her had jabbed a pencil into the place of the suffering in her hand. Her spiritual director, Monsignor George Habig, had to establish a rule that Rhoda would not be touched so as to spare her such aggravations of her normal "sufferings".)

We have today quite a few living stigmatists and victim souls. Some stigmatists will suffer many wounds of Christ such as from the Crown of Thorns or the Scourgings, others less. But, as a victim soul said to this author only a few days ago from this writing, it is largely the victim souls, stigmatists, etc., who hold the world together (by their reparational sufferings which avert or lessen the bolts and tribulations sent by God's Justice.) So was the world helped by the bloody tears and sweat of young Saint Gemma Galgani (1878-1903), the Passion Flower of Lucca, Italy, or, nearer our own times and place, the sufferings of Marie Rose Ferron (1902-1936) of Woonsocket, Rhode Island.

Padre Pio died some years ago, Martha Robin, a stigmatist of France a year or so ago, Teresa Musco of Caserta, Italy, a few years ago — and there were others. One can still visit living stigmatists like "Brother" Gino of San Vittorino near Rome. And Enzo Alocci at Porto San Stefano is a reputed stigmatist. Some, like Saint Catherine of Siena, have invisible stigmata (made so at her request). Outside of humility motives it might be more suitable for those leading a very active life. In our day, Barbara Reuss of Marienfried, Germany, apparently had invisible stigmata.

We have inserted this information concerning *living,* weeping, suffering *images of Christ,* of God, because, with all respect to the more common (these days) weeping and bleeding material images of Christ and Mary, animated to impress and inspire us, these chosen victim souls, stigmatists, portray *par excellence* the participatory and "salvific" sufferings, the reparational *love,* so imitative of that of Christ and Mary for us. A statue can weep and bleed and remind us of the realities in Christ and Mary. Statues cannot feel, suffer or love. Stigmatists and victim souls do all that!

At times stigmatists also have weeping images associated with them, and for persons close to such stigmatists, there is experienced a sort of "double-dip" of suffering manifestations presented to them. I think, however, that we can all understand, that if we cannot personally witness, (in *apparitions* or through a series of *visions*), the sufferings of Christ and Mary, their very tears, their blood, their excruciating agony, then the nearest thing to that is to witness it or visualize it (in imagination or through photos) in the persons, the anguished bodies and souls of the stigmatists and other victim souls.

These souls are indeed chosen, and no prudent, ordinary good Catholic will ask for the stigmata or mystical sufferings. The message, however, to us all is to offer up our own sufferings, to do some additional penances, sacrifices, mortifications, and to pray (the latter possible to all) for God's mercy and grace for all. It will be the supreme efforts of many "little" victim souls (see *Marguerite*) that will balance the scales and save the world.

The exceptional victim souls are the big weights to favor the balance. Here we might apply reparationally the old saying, let every one throw his or her own weight, spiritually, with love on the scale beside the heavyweights of our big Brother and Sister victim souls. Ten just men could have saved Sodom and Gomorrah and the other three cities destroyed with them. With all respect, if there had been "just men" in those old pagan cities, such men (or women) would have never approached the holiness of many New Testament Catholics much less that of stigmatists and victim souls. If we would look at the whole world today, in general, as a sort of Sodom and Gomorrah in its widespread evil, the importance and the weight of Christian victim souls will be more striking, and hopefully lead to more reparational love and suffering.

— D —

Our fourth group concerning tears and blood, the tear-shedding and bleeding images of Christ and Mary, we have seen at length. Since 1972, as the journalist, Alexander Permitzky is quoted in *Explosion of the Supernatural,* "It is like a flood of tears and blood over the world." Since he uttered those words some years back the flood of blood and tears has noticeably increased.

If you have not been so blessed — for the holy impressions made on you and the challenges given — as to see a victim soul writhing in suffering, or to visit (reverently and in a natural manner, but not curiously or skeptically) a well-established stigmatist, then read a good life of one or more and gaze at authentic photos of them in their sufferings. (See Bibliography: Johnston, *Alexandrina;* Spadafora-Cioffi, *Sister Elena Aiello;* Roschini, *Teresa Musco* — Italian, pictures in "English".)

The next nearest related experience to the classifications given above is to witness a genuine weeping (and best, a rather lengthy one for more surety and intake) of a sacred image of Christ or Mary. Or view authentic photographs of such tears on images, or listen to balanced and reputable witnesses and their accounts of the "tearings" and cryings they have personally seen. Especially those of blood, and, if possible, in color.

— E —

Finally, we mention the *tears* of the *ordinary people* (if we can use such a term as the latter). Recently, 1981, the Pilgrim Virgin statue (the

International Fatima one that wept at Las Vegas and has been recently, about the late summer of 1982, returned to Europe) was in the co-cathedral of Saint Joseph at Thibodaux, Louisiana. There must have been 2,000 or more persons venerating it one evening, including many pious and lovely dressed Vietnamese with their banners and own-language hymns. One American lady, that is a native citizen, looking on (kneeling) near this author, had tears rolling down her cheeks.

At actual weepings of her Fatima statues many people observing Mary's tears have wept their own in sympathy, or in realizing the sorrows of Mary and her Son over sin, and over the sufferings of the good. Many such witnesses have changed dramatically, have turned around their lives. People or priests who belittle "weeping statues" — and almost always have never witnessed an image of Mary crying — might open their eyes to such good fruits.

We are all called to share "daily" in the Way of the Cross. The tears and blood of Christ and Mary are not idle, curious or to be neglected matters. This is real life and death drama. The souls of millions are eternally at stake. When Christ appeared once to Sister Josefa Menéndez on February 4, 1921 He said to her: "Every Friday of the month, and especially on the First Friday of the month, I will cause you to share in the bitterness of My Heart's agony, and you will experience the torments of My Passion in a very particular manner."

Devotion to the Sacred Heart of Jesus is attractive and consoling, but real devotion goes deep and Josefa paid a heavy price to spread the devotion so many merely enjoy. When Christ appeared to Saint Margaret Mary, apostle of devotion to His Sacred Heart, He said to her:

"Every Thursday night I will make you share in that deathly sadness that I willingly endured in the Garden of Olives: this sadness will turn into a sort of agony, in a manner in which you will not be able to comprehend, an agony more painful to bear than death itself." — This concerned Margaret's consoling Christ by keeping Him company in His Agony by her making a sympathetic Holy Hour.

Most of us are not called to such intense and dreadful sufferings. Alas, we are not called to nor are able to rise to such love. However, let no individual zealous souls be discouraged! Let us do what we can and while time and opportunity for love and sacrifice remain. Pope John XXIII, elected in old age, said but little time was given him, but he meant to use that little time well. — yes, while but a *little* time remains!

Let us be consoled in our various sufferings of reparation and love with the fact that Christ and Mary too have "suffered" with the sufferings of their helper victim souls. Mary has *wept* over *their* sufffer-ings in motherly sympathy, consolation and encouragement.

Our tears are Mary's tears, as they are also her Son's. And their tears are our tears.

Saint Paul wrote to the Corinthians: "That is why I wrote you in great sorrow and anguish, with copious tears — not to make you sad but to help you realize the great love I bear you." (2 Cor. 2:4)

So, too, the tears of Christ and Mary — and their love for man-kind!

We must extend that love, especially to the poor, the innocent and the ignorant. As a wise man of the Old Testament wrote long ago:

"Again I considered all the oppressions that take place under the sun: the tears of the victims with none to comfort them." (Eccl. 4:1)

"O all ye who come by the way! Is there any sorrow like unto My sorrow!"

Medal of Our Lady of America

XVIII — THE HOLY FATHER, MOTHER CHURCH AND SURVIVAL

"I have heard your prayer and seen your tears." **2 Kgs. 20:5.**

The Holy Father has been mentioned in prophecies in connection with Italy. The Church and the Pope, of course, are intimately connected, and Sister Elena Aiello has additional warnings or prophecies concerning both the Holy Father and the Church.

(The author should state here that he is indebted to the life of Sister Elena Aiello, to Florence Cioffi, the sister of the translator of that volume, and to the publication *Divine Love*. The book has an imprimatur and all articles in *Divine Love* are cleared first through the Diocesan Censor.)

There is nothing new about such prophetical warnings. It is not our purpose here to speak of the many reliable prophecies dealing with the sufferings of Church and Pope. Such were those of Venerable Katerine Emmerick, Blessed Anna Maria Taigi, others, and especially our Lady at Fatima. And Jacinta of Fatima. The obvious connection, however, between weeping Fatima statues, basic Fatima messages and similar prophecies cannot be overlooked.

To fill out what we have already heard from Sister Elena Aiello about Italy and the Church, we add here a few other prophetic utterances received through her, and concerning the Pope.

On Good Friday, April 7, 1950, Sister Elena asked Mary: "What will become of Italy? Will Rome be saved?"

"In part, by the Pope," Mary answered. "The Church will be in travail, but the forces of Hell cannot prevail! You must suffer for the Pope and Christ, and thus Christ will be safe on earth; and the Pope, with his redemptive word, will, in part, save the world."

Speaking on Good Friday, March 23, 1951, Mary said her heart bled for Italy and added: "Oh! what grief to see the representative of Christ on earth hated, persecuted, outraged!"

Speaking on December 8, 1956, Mary said: "The Pope will suffer much, and all this suffering will be like an agony, which will shorten his earthly pilgrimage. His successor will guide the boat in the tempest."

Some interpreters would say, the popes referred to are Paul VI and John Paul II. Others might place the prophecies on John Paul II and his successor.

In 1959 Mary said: "The flock is about to be dispersed and the Pope must suffer greatly."

On Good Friday, 1960, Mary said: "In these tragic hours, the world has need of prayers and penance, because the pope, the priests, and the Church are in danger. Russia will march upon all of Europe, and particularly on Italy, bringing much more ruin and havoc."

On Good Friday, 1961: "The Church will be persecuted and the Pope and the priests shall suffer much."

Then Sister Elena spoke of a vision shown her: "Oh, what a horrible vision I see! A great revolution is going on in Rome! They are entering the Vatican. The Pope is all alone, he is praying. They are holding the Pope. They take him by force. They knock him down to the floor. They are tying him. Oh, God! Oh, God! They are kicking him. What a horrible scene! How dreadful!"

"Our Blessed Mother is drawing near. Like corpses those evil men fall down to the floor. Our Lady helps the Pope to his feet, and, taking him by the arms, she covers him with her mantle, saying, "Fear not!"

Jacinta of Fatima, July 13, 1917, sitting on the stone slabs on top of the well, had this vision: "I saw the Holy Father in a very big house, kneeling by a table, with his head buried in his hands, and he was weeping. Outside the house, there were many people. Some of them were throwing stones, others were cursing him and using bad language. Poor Holy Father, we must pray much for him." (*Lucia Speaks — Memoirs* . . . p. 133, AMI Press.)

Saint John Bosco saw a similar scene with the Pope in danger and two men at his side. The young American mother mentioned earlier claims a vision scene where Italy is invaded by Russia and two men, in unidentifiable uniforms but uniforms representing an evil force, are threatening the present Holy Father. They seemed to represent an evil force trying to push the Holy Father, John Paul II, out of the Vatican. One man held a gun to the Pope's head. (Not the 1982 assassination attempt.)

What then, in the present circumstances, can the Church do, especially the Holy Father and its high ranking members? And what can all Church members do to safeguard and help the Holy Father? The whole matter is complex, but we shall try to put forth some simple but important helpful actions that can be taken.

First, regarding the dangers Mary forecast at Fatima: "If my requests are granted, Russia will be converted and there will be peace. If not, Russia will spread her errors in every country. raising up wars and persecutions against the Church; many will be martyred. The Holy Father will have much to suffer, and several nations will be destroyed."

Much forecast in those prophetic words has already transpired. One can expect other tribulations to come, such as more persecution of the Church and the Holy Father (not just physical), and, probably, a Third World War; and possibly a nuclear one at that. Even another widespread war with the latest "conventional weapons" would be terribly devastating.

As one of her conditions for the conversion of Russia and world peace, Mary asked that the Holy Father with all the bishops of the world would consecrate Russia to the Immaculate Heart of Mary. It would seem, at the time of this revised writing, that this Consecration, at least to some extent, was made by Pope John Paul II at Fatima, May 13, 1982. Lucy considers it so but said it was *late*. She also said that much would depend upon the response of the world to that May 13 Consecration and upon the work of the Blue Army.

The collegial consecration was asked for by Mary in an apparition in the chapel of the Dorothean Sisters in Tuy, Spain, 1929. Our Lady said then: "Now is the time when God asks the Holy Father, in union with all the bishops of the world, to make the consecration of Russia to my Immaculate Heart, promising to save it by this means." That request for "now" in 1929 was over fifty years ago. To this author and some other persons, it would seem, while the Holy Father did his part on May 13, 1982 with Lucy present, that there could have been a much better evident response and participation by the bishops "collegially" throughout the world.

The Bishops were informed, it would seem certain, but how many actually made a public consecration of Russia to Mary's Immaculate Heart with the Pope, though distant, on that date? The Consecration seems to have been incomplete in this respect. It would seem very practical and a matter of relief to many (if also considered "ideal" by others) if the Holy Father would renew the May 13, 1982 Consecration on some significant date announced long before and with the Bishops ordered or instructed to collegially co-consecrate Russia to the Immaculate Heart of Mary, in their cathedrals, at the same solar time or calendar date.

It would seem that a Vatican II session of the Bishops from throughout the world, along with the Pope then, would have been an ideal time and setting for such a consecration. Nothing would be hurt by the Consecration we have suggested but only tremendous good gained. We cannot wait for another General Council of the Church. The world situation is extremely urgent!

Regarding bishops in general, they, especially bishop-ordinaries in some cases, need prayers and encouragement to support more actively genuine manifestations of the supernatural, of which there are many. True, some bishops may be flooded with reports of alleged apparitions, miracles, etc., some of which are false. The bishops are very busy and should be. But, as Haffert states in *Explosion of the Supernatural,* "As the authors of *Segno dei Tempi* (Sign of Our Times)," responsible writers, "point out, many bishops seem reluctant to take a positive stand on many of these phenomena."

Note that "positive stand". If it's going to be condemnatory, unless heresy is involved, in some cases at least it might prove wiser to say nothing.

Thorough canonical investigations and early affirmations of genuine supernatural phenomena and authentic happenings would greatly encourage the people to fulfill the urgent and vital requests made by Our Lord and Our Lady. Matters in many such instances could at least be termed seemingly credible, if also hedged with protective episcopal statements as to the necessity of obedience to any further or final judgments. And such judgments, especially early, premature local ones, one way or the other, positive or negative, are not infallible. That does not mean they are not to be respected, but, in a word, are still reversible.

Nor do such positive statements or judgments need to affirm or approve *all* reported manifestations, messages, claims or details, but only what is clearly inexplicable by natural causes and what is the substantial and credible message content.

Such procedures would also remove the fears, and in some cases substantiated fears, that in a climate of downgrading the supernatural today, of being "frightened" or embarrassed by private revelations and the miraculous, etc., attitudes and judgments of certain ecclesiastics may be affected overmuch by *a priori* opinions, prejudices and even a well-meant but false and unfortunate zeal of protectiveness.

In such cases where negative judgments are given (remember, we are dealing here with a good number of far-spread dioceses in various nations), it would seem that the faithful should be given the rationale and the main facts of procedures, plus the findings that support negative judgments; but also those on the positive side, as in any court of evidence.

This would seem particularly in order where there are authentic photographs and positive laboratory reports concerning tears, fluids or blood of weeping images, and where claimed cures and other apparent supernatural favors are involved. Also where unusual knowledge has been exhibited and prophecies made have already been fulfilled.

All this is positively and favorably augmented where there has resulted an obvious and great amount of spiritual good: the conversion of sinners and unbelievers, a return to the Sacraments, the renewal of Christian life and the enfiring of virtue, sacrifice and even heroic Catholic apostolates in certain individuals.

The Bishops of Sicily are to be commended when, in less than a year, that hierarchial group concluded their investigations and pronounced the weeping Madonna of Syracuse (Siracusa, Sicily) a genuine phenomenon inexplicable naturally, whereupon the construction of the great basilica-shrine there had its beginnings. Admittedly, all cases of alleged miracles may not be as "simple" to handle in some respects. But they can be determined in their vital and important elements.

It is not necessary, for instance, to declare anything about the moral and spiritual life, about the holiness of a person or "instrument" involved in the matter of a weeping statue. The *facts*, however, of such weepings should be admitted. Further judgments might be withheld with regard to prophecies being fulfilled (often contingent upon human response made to specific requests), or to the content of messages or private revelations claimed. Miracles, however, are good back-up signs of such claims, especially repeated ones or sequences of them.

If, however, there has been a proven sequence of weepings, what harm can come from recommending a message-content that says doing good, that penance, prayer and reparation are needed?

It is this author's experience from contacts with many persons who have witnessed cryings of sacred images, that out of hearts many thoughts are revealed. The mere seeing of or knowledge of weepings (or through photos of them) brings out, for the most part — except for the few incurable skeptics — various responses of good. Such are the good fruits! As indicated earlier, the tears of one's Mother or Saviour bring some kind of healthy response from ordinary human beings. Let the people then be exposed to such tears, whether witnessed in apparitions by mystics or seen by ordinary people when sacred images weep them vicariously for Christ and His Mother.

We might conclude here with a summary of what is generally requested by Christ and His Mother in apparently genuine apparitions (a number already favorably received or approved by the Church) or alleged ones that some persons might doubt. I do not think anyone will find any heresy or error in any of them. All these requests only accent by unusual manifestations before human witnesses what the Church regularly favors or teaches:

1) The living of a good Christian life. accent on Gospel living and daily duties.

2) Prayer, penance, sacrifices and reparation for sinners and sin.

3) Eucharistic devotion, especially by Holy Hours, visits to the Blessed Sacrament and vigils. First Friday and First Saturday Mass and Communion.

4) Individual consecration to the Sacred Heart of Jesus and to the Immaculate Heart of Mary. Consecration of Russia to the Immaculate Heart of Mary, by the Holy Father and all the bishops collegially, and the living of that Consecration.

5) Recitation of the Rosary daily, if possible the fifteen decades, with meditation on the mysteries. Also the Family Rosary.

6) Wearing of the Brown Scapular and proper devotion to Our Lady of Mount Carmel.

7) Purity, and practice of Christian modesty in dress.

8) Support of and loyalty to the Holy Father, and orthodox doctrine.

These requests are not very hard to meet. Yet the spiritual and temporal welfare of the world depend upon their fulfillment. The Mercy and Justice of God hang in the balance. Human response to the pleas of Christ and Mary are vital — and urgent! (It is suggested that one read here the basic Fatima messages given in an appendix.)

Finally, it might be suggested that individual dioceses, parishes, religious orders, communities, organizations and families all consecrate their membership and Russia to the Immaculate Heart of Mary. That would really be a total knocking at the doors of heaven!

> "We have come as a humble and faithful pilgrim to this holy sanctuary . . ." — Paul VI, May 13, 1967 at Fatima.

XIX — THE JACINTA 1972 "PROPHECY" AND 1972

"weeping so that her tears fell upon His feet." **Lk. 7:44**

Some years ago many people were taken up with the prophecy or caution of little Jacinta of Fatima concerning 1972. Jacinta when sick and when in the hospital toward the end of her short life spoke of a number of things. While very ill she was in the orphanage of Mother Godinho in Lisbon before being taken to the hospital where she died. Mother Godinho recorded a number of the little seer's wise sayings. Among them was the "prophecy" regarding 1972.

This was over sixty years ago as Jacinta died February 20, 1920. Mother Godinho kept this prophecy a secret until, fearing her end was drawing near, she wrote Pope Pius XII about it in a letter of April 25, 1954. The letter was subsequently printed in the September-October issue of the Portuguese review, *Mensagem de Fatima (Message of Fatima).*

Mother Godinho, under oath, assured the Pope that these were Jacinta's words "Godmother [the orphans called the nun "godmother"], tell the Holy Father that the world is in a turmoil and that Our Lady can no longer hold back the arm of Her Beloved Son, greatly offended by the sins that are being committed in the world."

There was more said about penance or punishment. Our concern here, however, is that Mother Godinho then said that Jacinta begged Mother Godinho that the Sisters of her order would always remain united with the Vatican, "and that", as Mother Godinho told it, "they should prepare themselves for the year 1972 because the sins of impurity and of vanity and of excessive luxury would bring upon the world such punishments that they will cause much suffering to the Holy Father."

These words and other things Jacinta said at that time led many people to surmise that something unusual would happen before or in 1972, punishment, chastisement and/or the triumph of Mary of the Immaculate Heart.

We might point out here that at times important world events are actually happening, or in the making, and we scarcely notice it. For instance, certain persons had some difficulty about the Fatima prophecy that World War II would begin in the reign of a designated pontiff, a certain pope. The simple answer to the apparent problem was that the War actually had begun with Hitler's early moves and particularly with the Nazi occupation of Austria.

Let us look, however, at some of the most significant happenings in 1972, merely considering the spiritual and supernatural events and ignoring natural disasters of which many occurred around that time.

In 1972, as we have seen, there occurred an unusual number of weepings of sacred images, especially of *Fatima* statues. This was true of both Italy and the United States. Indeed, in the United States the weepings of the North American International Pilgrim Virgin Fatima statue crescendoed toward the latter half of the year to famous weepings at New Orleans, Atlanta, and in a New York town. Further, a second Fatima statue, that of the lady in a previous chapter, began to weep often and copiously in September 1972.

Another significant spiritual event was the inspiration for the Marian Movement of Priests at Fatima in May 1972, a very important movement, along with its associated book, *Our Lady Speaks to Her Beloved Priests.*

What then is a possible explanation for these happenings and activities in relation to the words of Jacinta "to be prepared" (at least for that particular order of Sisters) by 1972. Of course, the interpretation of many persons was that it meant, the "prophecy", that something unusual or important was to happen, and that it would affect many people more or less.

The intelligent person knows that external manifestations or effects must be attributed to some cause. It was no accident then that so many weepings and other unusual events (we could add more of them) took place in 1972. In the United States at least it is easier to be informed of events and to follow the developments which became urgent in the latter months of 1972.

To make it brief, besides all that happened in Italy alone, the Blessed Mother was almost "feverish" in her attempts, in the United States, to get across a message of needed prayer, penance, Eucharistic adoration, and reparation. People may form their own opinions, but no one can get around all the miraculous weepings of Marian statues then, particularly the weepings of the two famous Fatima ones. This is a matter of recent history and has its meaning.

What is our choice? If we were to attribute so many witnessed, photographed and lengthy weepings of sacred images of the Mother of God, to the devil, then the Church will be in an impossible situation regarding the authoritative declaration of any genuine miracles. No miracle will then be able to stand, in the Bible or otherwise, and no miracle will be able to be used apologetically to prove the authenticity and divinity of Christ's Holy Catholic Church.

Nor is this author aware that any bishop or responsible person has claimed such weepings to be of diabolical origin. So, we must face the fact, particularly in view of the many good spiritual fruits that ensued, that these weepings were truly miraculous, and that they were allowed or worked by God. Then, as any good theologian should know, such signs endorse special missions or messages connected with them and which are claimed as authentic by the "instruments" employed by God to transmit them. (We recommend a reading of chapters 4 and 5 on the Christian miracle and Christian life in Monden's *Signs and Wonders.*)

Christ Himself asked His enemies or doubters to at least believe in the works that accompanied His teaching.

In the United States then, in the latter half of 1972, the North American International Pilgrim Virgin Fatima statue, which represented ambassadorially Our Lady's message at Fatima, after numerous other weepings, some with striking timings, as at the time of the Attica Prison Riot deaths in September 1971 and the Rapid City flood disaster in June 1972, wept twice at New Orleans, then at Atlanta, and then in New York State.

Further, when this statue became disengaged from the lady in whose presence it had so often wept, "AW", a lady who claimed to have a special mission and messages backed up by those weepings in her presence, then the weepings shifted almost immediately to another beautiful Fatima statue sent to her. This statue was from Portugal and privately owned by a doctor and his wife for about two years, without any cryings, and given by them to the lady in September 1972, under special circumstances.

More, the weepings of this second Fatima statue were preceded by about eight weepings of an Immaculate Conception Lourdes type statue of Mary given to the same lady by another doctor and his wife. These latter weepings occurred in the interim between the North American International Pilgrim Virgin statue weepings and those of the new Fatima statue weepings.

At the heightening period of these weepings, in October 1972 the Blessed Virgin reputedly declared, and so the lady proclaimed it then of Mary:

"I have buried them in signs!"

Indeed, will someone inform us, where and when has there been such a sequence of weepings in the history of the world? And we might add, and when such a miracle as the spinning sun miracle at Fatima? Did Our Lord not ask long ago, "Can you not read the signs of the times?" — most unusual signs!

When this unusual sequence of Fatima weepings, especially in the context of the prominence, fame and purpose of the International Fatima Pilgrim statue to North America, were at their height the lady, "AW", was stating that the message she was "transmitting" was the overall and over-riding reason for all these weepings. The basic message was that, because of so much sin in the world, reparation was urgently needed, Eucharistic adoration, penance, prayer, rosary, etc., or mankind faced great tribulations. It is not our purposes to go into the sources of her declarations here. We are trying to throw light on the 1972 year "puzzle", and the lady threw light on it long ago.

This lady declared then that a time, a year for a "judgment" had come. So many appeals had been made by Christ and Mary for reform over many years (Fatima itself went back to 1917) and the world had not responded sufficiently to date. The world was being given a last chance for prevention of certain great trials and tribulations due for the sins of the world, indeed overdue.

If this demand for reparation was not sufficiently met by the end of 1972, then a "judgment" would be made. Because of this judgment, there could be a moral certainty on men's part, as it were, that these promised chastisements would gradually unfold. This did not mean that unusual things would happen right on January 1, 1973, mathematically, or just after.

Rather, as in a court case when a judgment is rendered, the fulfilling of the sentence in its details would come later, so with such prophesied events. Nor did it mean that whatsover chastisement, tribulation, punishment, were adjudged for the future, that they could not be lessened, modified or prevented in a particular area or for certain people, by continued or increased reparational efforts.

Some persons may have the opinion, and it is that of this author, merely private, that all this involves the unfolding of the Third Secret of Fatima. This approach, too, because of the signs of the times and other privileged sources, was employed by this lady years ago, long before it was stated in print by another apparent special instrument of God, a well-known priest.

In a word, it would now seem that we can have a moral certainty of the fulfilling of the "if" contingent prophecies of Our Lady of Fatima. Indeed, we can so determine from many other sources, genuine seers, mystics, victim souls, stigmatists, prophets, that these prophecies of Fatima concerning great troubles, persecution, sufferings of the Holy Father, the evils of Communism, and even annihilation of whole nations in nuclear war will see fulfillment, or further fulfillment before long. (We must note there can also be a moral annihilation of nations and that the more vital war, that over souls, a great spiritual conflict, has been going on and increasing for some time.)

Hope, however, can always shine before us, especially for individual good people or certann wholesome areas. Indeed, the very fact that we can consider that a judgment has been made (and of course this is individual responsibility or opinion — look however to the developing facts!), should quicken and energize all people to all-out efforts of reparational activity. The appreciative mercy of God and intercession of Mary Mediatrix of all graces will lessen and moderate, if nothing else, those many trials usually headed under the prophetic designations of "the great tribulation", "chastisement" or "purification". Christ and Mary have told us this through an overwhelming number of holy souls.

For instance, Jesus reportedly has promised certain things through Sister Claire Ferchaud of Loublande, France as the Merciful Saviour with a Broken Heart: "I come, not to bring terror among you; I am the God of Love, the God Who forgives and wants to save you all." And, "My grace will work with great power on sinners who without contrition, kneel before the picture of My Broken Heart, so that they will arise converted."

Without a doubt, then, the eventual triumph of the Immaculate Heart of Mary, as she also promised at Fatima, and an era of the reign of Christ over hearts will take place. A number of reliable "seers", as far as this author is concerned (including reportedly Lucy of Fatima) are credited with seeing light at the end of the tunnel and the coming victory of the Immaculate Heart of Mary and an era of peace. But the immediate future will be a time of urgency as we face increasing troubles. The evils in the world are unfolding them!

Practically speaking, for anyone surveying the world since 1972, all kinds of increasing disasters, physical, economic, political, religious can be noted. Also the sad divisions within the Church, the general corruption of morals, especially in the areas of sex, marriage and family life, drugs, alcoholism, disbelief, atheism, etc. Then we have widespread crime increase, revolutionary and subversive activities, and assassination attempts on the most prominent world leaders. The world is sick and sick in its own vomit!

One of the greatest disasters, however, in the United States alone, hardly considered so by many (a further disaster!), and right after the year 1972 ended, was the United States Supreme Court's abortion ruling. If 50,000 American boys would have died in a war in 1973, say in a six week period, that would have been considered as a great fulfillment of the above "judgment" declarations. Yet a million American babies (who should have been future American citizens) in the womb were destroyed within a year of that ruling. And ten to fifteen million American babies since! If that is not one of the greatest — and continuing — disasters in world and American history, what then has been or is? And it cries to heaven for vengeance.

We are certainly also experiencing spiritual disasters which are much worse for mankind than disease, famine or physical death. Besides evils mentioned above, child pornography alone is enough to invite the wrath of God Who warned against scandalizing His little ones. The millstones and the sea await these offenders! Sodom and Gomorrah are all around us and justfied as a moral style of life. And some are becoming more and more involved in the old pagan, degrading practice of vomiting their food repeatedly or otherwise disposing of it so as to have the mere pleasure alone of eating again and again. Other "vomitoriums" are all around us.

We are become like a people with a slow pollution gathering around us. We hardly realize that our civilization is in danger of absolute contamination and death. It is a creeping evil engulfing us, a silent cancer penetrating to our very bones.

Today World War III hangs over mankind and the world is in a near paralysis of fear on one part and in a feverish activity of arms-building on the other. It may happen, War, before we know it — may God forbid! But the sins of the world call for the punishment of war, and men bring on their own punishments. Disasters loom which they could so easily prevent by personal conversion and leading good lives, by reparation and penance, by a little love of God and Man.

It is the opinion then of this author, that the many weepings, the sheddings of salt and blood tears, the "bleedings", the appeals of Christ and Mary in 1972 indicated that 1972 was indeed a special year. More, that all the people living since then have had to guard against increasing moral evils of all sorts. That, on the happier side, there are columns of good people, forces of sound and healthy spiritual movements, in particular of the reparational type, that are stirring in remedial action.

There will be an increasing confrontation between the forces of good and evil. There is going on and there will continue a great purification process. There will be eventual defeat for Satan and the evil forces aligned with him. Saint Michael and the good angels will help usher in the triumph of Mary and her Son. The prayers of the saints and of the martyred will not go unanswered.

After this triumphal period of peace, the author would be of the opinion, from many readings, that the world will see the advent of the Antichrist, a person of arch-evil, much persecution and the real battle of Armageddon. After that will come an uncertain period of time, and the final battle between good and evil, the days of Gog and Magog, the End of the World and Judgment. These opinions are given in a general way with the renewed assertion that the Calendar of God is not the calendar of men. But it is a Calendar relentlessly unfolding until the times of the nations are fulfilled and the Day of the Lord has come.

The practical thing for anyone to do is to fall in line whole-heartedly with the requests that Christ and Mary have made through so many instruments in our time, and through so many tears of salt and of blood. When we see blood flowing from the Heart of Mary, if vicarously so through her image, from the Head and wounds of Christ, even from the umbilical-cord navel area of the Innocent Baby Jesus (the Bambino of Christmas Life and Love), then we know Christ and Mary have exhausted their appeals to our sanity and our own love.

The sun continues to spin as it were over Fatima, Mary walks in the brilliant light of her reality above the Coptic Church in Cairo, and prophets and seers trumpet their messages of mercy and warnings of chastisement. We are amidst some of the most unusual manifestations in history. In our own lifetime! The world indeed had better wake up! Or a good part of it may find itself destroyed overnight. "As in the days of Noah . . ." "As in the days of Lot, Sodom and Gomorrah . . ."

For rejecting the blood and tears of the innocent Christ, of the Immaculate Heart of Mary!

(A final note: It must be accented here that there are numerous prophecies current in the United States and worldwide prophecies spoken of in the Charismatic Movement that forecast the imminent time of tribulation and purification to affect the Church and the world.)

> "He will lead them to springs of life-giving water, and God will wipe every tear from their eyes." — Rev. 7:17

Having spoken of Jacinta of Fatima, of Fatima and Fatima statues so much it would be suitable to offer some praise of the Blue Army here. The Blue Army of Our Lady of Fatima should be credited with a great spread of the Fatima message and devotion. Its sponsoring of Pilgrim Virgin statues and encouragement of the veneration of Fatima statues in general have provided the base for the weepings of International and National Pilgrim Virgin statues. Of course, the Lord and Mary have also made use of other Fatima statues, as we have seen. God is not limited. The scope of the missions of Christ and Mary embraces many modern movements within the Church and various persons who have been chosen as special instruments of God and Mary.

It is very important that all these movements and privileged persons work together to achieve God's Overall Will. Individuals should never fall into the temptation to let their own will and work substitute for the Will and the Works of God. Nor should anyone engage in unseemly, even unChristian competition or interchanges, or cause divisions, all of which conduct is the work of the devil and most harmful to the true good that God Himself intends.

Pope John Paul II, recuperating after assassination attempt.

OUR LADY OF TEARS

Our Lady of Tears, why do you weep?
Your tears have coursed your cheeks
from the eyes of your sacred images,
Immaculate Heart, Fatima, Queen of the World,
wet, salty, beautiful tear-droplets —
Lady, why do you weep?

You have wept at Syracuse,
you have cried again and again:
at Ravenna, at Caserta,
at Porto San Stefano, San Vittorino;
even blood has flowed from your innocent eyes,
and, incomprehensibly, your Immaculate Heart —
Lady, Mother, why do you weep?

In Haiti, as the National *Fatima*
Pilgrim Virgin, you cried in that land,
as in that of Syria you teared at Damascus.
As the North American Pilgrim Virgin
you wept copiously in New Orleans,
and then cried in Atlanta and in New York —
Mary, you have soaked cloths with your tears!
Have you rebuked us with your signs and your sighs,
Do you weep over mankind with compassion and love?
Lady, why is your face so sad, why do you cry?

Through the eyes of a second International
Pilgrim Virgin, you wept at Las Vegas,
several times — thousands, the mayor saw it.
Do we ask why, just before you toured the world,
and the Communist general would not let you enter
the land of the Holy Father, martyred Poland
of your sword-slashed image of Our Lady of Jasna Gora?

Lady, why do you weep?
You have wept through your Fatima images
many other times, some times tearing for hours,
or again and again: at Chicago, Pittsburgh, Wheeling,
at Agawam, Kenner, Commack, at hamlet or farm —
Lady, who has heard of it, who has told it,
who has heeded or wept at your sobs and your sorrows?
Your tears well up in your eyes, your lids redden;

they trickle down your nose, hang in droplets
from your chin, fall on your breast, wet the floor;
portent? — they run over the globe held in your hands!

Our Lady of Tears, why do you weep, why sorrowfully
even shed blood from your Pure and Immaculate Heart?
Why through so many images of you of Fatima,
of the miracle of the spinning and hurtling sun?
Lady, Mother, *Our Lady of Fatima,* why do you weep?

— the Author in *Mary Our Blessed Mother*

Crucifix corpus (of "CE") with ordinary tear.

Notes

1. Poulain, S.J., A., *Graces of Interior Prayer*, Celtic Cross Books, Westminster, VT. (1978) p. 349.
2. Garrigou-LaGrange, O.P., Rev. R., *The Three Ages of the Interior Life*, Vol. Two, B. Herder Bk. Co., St. Louis, MO. (1948), p. 580.
3. *Op. cit.*, p. 349.
4. *Op. cit.*, p. 581.
5. Rahner, S.J., Karl, *Visions and Prophecies*, Herder and Herder, N.Y. (1963), p. 18.
6. Poulain, op. cit., pp. 349-350.
7. Rahner, op. cit., p. 23.
8. Arintero, O.P., John G., *The Mystical Evolution in the Development and Vitality of the Church*, tr. by Fr. Jordan Aumann, O.P., Tan Books and Publishers, Inc., Rockford, IL. (1978) Vol. 2, p. 305.
9. Monden, S.J., Louis, *Signs and Wonders*, Desclee Co., N.Y. (1966), p. 94.

Syrian National Pilgrim Virgin weeping, Damascus, July, 1977

APPENDIX A

All that has been presented in this book can be centered around these private revelations of Our Lady at Fatima:

"Now, when you say the Rosary, add after each decade the following prayer: 'Oh, my Jesus, forgive us our sins. Save us from the fire of Hell and lead all souls to Heaven, especially those who have most need of Your Mercy.' "

To Lucy: "God wishes to use you to make me known and loved, to establish throughout the world devotion to my Immaculate Heart. To all those who embrace it I promise salvation and their souls will be loved by God as flowers placed by me before His throne."

— June 13, 1917.

"Continue to come every month. In October I will tell you who I am and will work a miracle so great that all will believe in the reality of the apparitions. Sacrifice yourselves for poor sinners and say this prayer very often: Oh, my Jesus, it is for love of You, for the conversion of sinners and in reparation for all the wrongs done to the Immaculate Heart of Mary."

After the vision of Hell: "You have seen Hell where the souls of sinners go. To save them, God wishes to establish in the world the devotion to my Immaculate Heart. If people do as I shall ask, many souls will be converted and there will be peace. This War (World War I) is going to end, but if people do not cease offending God, not much time will elapse and during the Pontificate of Pius XI another and more terrible war will begin. When you shall see a night illumined by an unknown light, know that this is the great sign that God gives (January 25, 1938 according to Lucy) that the chastisement of the world for its many transgressions is at hand through war, famine, persecution of the Church and of the Holy Father.

"To prevent this, I shall come to ask for the consecration of Russia to my Immaculate Heart and the Communion of reparation on the first Saturdays. If my requests are heard, Russia will be converted and there will be peace. If not, she will spread her errors throughout the entire world, fomenting wars and persecution of the Church. The good will suffer martyrdom; the Holy Father will suffer much; different nations will be annihilated. But in the end my Immaculate Heart shall triumph. The Holy Father will consecrate Russia to me, which will be converted and some time of peace will be granted to humanity!"

— July 13, 1917.

"Pray, pray very much and make sacrifices for sinners, for many souls go to Hell because there is no one to make sacrifices for them."

— August 19, 1917.

Regarding the sick: "I will cure some of them but not all, because the Lord has no confidence in them."

— September 13, 1917.

"I am the Lady of the Rosary. People must amend their lives, ask pardon for their sins and not offend Our Lord any more, for He is already too much offended."

Then came the great miracle of the spinning and hurtling sun.

— October 13, 1917.

Through every month from May to October Mary asked for the Rosary to be prayed in these or similar words: "Pray the Rosary every day . . ." (May) and "Continue to pray the Rosary every day." (October)

In her last appearance on October 13, 1917, and in her very last apparition then, Mary appeared as Our Lady of Mount Carmel and holding the Scapular in her hand.

"In 1946 I crowned Our Lady of Fatima (through a Legate) Queen of the World and the following year, through the Pilgrim Virgin, She set forth to claim her dominion . . . and the favors She performs along the way are such that We can hardy believe what we are seeing with our eyes." — Pope Pius XII.

On one's knees at Fatima

APPENDIX B

It would seem suitable to append here the "Prayer to the Immaculate Conception" connected with the Our Lady of America private revelations:

"O Immaculate Mother, Queen of our Country, open our hearts, our homes, and our Land to the coming of Jesus, your Divine Son. With Him, reign over us, O heavenly Lady, so pure and so bright with the radiance of God's light shining in and about you. Be our Leader against the powers of evil set upon wrestling the world of souls, redeemed at such a great cost by the sufferings of your Son and of yourself, in union with Him, from that same Savior, Who loves us with infinite charity.

We gather about you, O chaste and holy Mother, Virgin Immaculate, Patroness of our beloved Land, determined to fight under your banner of holy purity against the wickedness that would make all the world an abyss of evil, without God and without your loving maternal care.

We consecrate our hearts, our homes, our Land to your Most Pure Heart, O great Queen, that the kingdom of your Son, our Redeemer and our God, may be firmly established in us.

We ask no special sign of you, sweet Mother, for we believe in your great love for us, and we place in you our entire confidence. We promise to honor you by faith, love, and the purity of our lives according to your desire.

Reign over us, then, O Virgin Immaculate, with your Son Jesus Christ. May His Divine Heart and your most chaste Heart be ever enthroned and glorified among us. Use us, your children of America, as your instruments in bringing peace among men and nations. Work your miracles of grace in us, so that we may be a glory to the Blessed Trinity, Who created, redeemed, and sanctifies us.

May your valiant Spouse, St. Joseph, with the holy Angels and saints, assist you and us in "renewing the face of the earth." Then when our work is over, come, Holy Immaculate Mother, and as our Victorious Queen, lead us to the eternal kingdom, where your Son reigns forever as King."

We add the invocation prayer that Mary taught Sister M. and which Mary wished engraved on the medal. One can find it on the side-rims of one face of the medal which has a picture of Mary as She appeared to Sister M., September 26, 1956 as Our Lady of America:

"By thy Holy and Immaculate Conception, O Mary,
deliver us from evil."

Other scroll aspirations on the reverse of the medal are:
Gloria Patri et Filio et Spiritui Sancto
Jesus, Maria, Joseph!

The Immaculate Conception prayer has the imprimatur of Paul F. Leibold, Vicar General of Cincinnati, later Archbishop.

Artist's representation of "Our Lady of America"

APPENDIX C

It is of interest to note that there is devotion to Our Lady under the title of Our Lady of Tears. Associated with the devotion are a special rosary of Our Lady of Tears, a picture and a medal. This devotion, however, was founded prior to the modern or late large number of Marian apparitions and weeping Marian images. It seems a very appropriate devotion for our times.

This devotion came about with private revelations of the Blessed Mother to Sister Amalia of Jesus Scourged, a holy nun of the Institute of the Crucified Jesus for Women Missionaries in Campinas, Brazil. She was a stigmatist. The picture shows Mary with ten crosses running down the front of her robe or tunic, and holding in her two lowered outstretched hands a seven decade rosary of seven small pearls each with seven larger dividing pearls, all of same color, white. The rosary is similar to that of the Seven Sorrows of Mary.

Attached to the rosary is a medal of Our Lady of Tears and three small pearls. The medal must be an exact duplicate of the one revealed to Sister Amalia by Mary on April 8, 1930. This medal is an essential part of the rosary. The arrangement recalls the sorrows over which Mary shed so many tears. (Now, we might add, Mary has many new sorrows!) In reciting the rosary of Our Lady of Tears the Apostles' Creed, Our Father and Hail Mary are not said (this rosary is not a substitution for the official rosary of Mary, but a pious devotion like many other rosaries are).

In place of the Creed is said: "Crucified Jesus! Prostrate at Your feet we offer You the tears of Her who accompanied You with ardent, sympathetic love on Your sorrowful way to the Cross. Grant, O good Master, that we may take to heart Your teachings which have given us the tears of Your most Holy Mother, so that we may fulfill Your Holy Will on earth in order to be made worthy to honor and praise You in Heaven throughout Eternity."

In place of the Our Father: "V. O Jesus! Behold the tears of Her who loved You most on earth. R. And loves You most ardently in Heaven." In place of the Hail Mary: "O, Jesus, hear our prayers. R. For the sake of the tears of Your Most Holy Mother." At the conclusion of the decades repeat three times, using the small beads: "O, Jesus! Look upon the tears of her who loved You most on earth and loves You most ardently in Heaven."

After the last three invocations the final prayer is recited: "O Mary, Mother of Love, of Sorrow and Compassion! We beg you, join your prayers with ours, so that Jesus, your Divine Son to Whom we turn, may hear our supplications in the name of your motherly tears and grant us the peace we so ardently seek so that we may obtain the crown of eternal life. Amen."

The above devotion involves statement or imprimatur of Msgr. Count Franciscus of Campos Barreto, Bishop of Campinas, and Michael J. Gallagher, Bishop of Detroit. As Bishop Franciscus is reported saying: "When torments, anxieties and pain fill our hearts, let us lift our thoughts to God. By the Tears of Mary, His most Holy Mother, we will make His Divine Heart gentle, even though it is ever ready to grant clemency, mercy and blessings. At the present time, it would seem, the Holy Tears of the Mother of Jesus are most powerful in touching the Heart of God." — These words written some years ago certainly apply today!

Countless favors have been attributed to the above devotion involving sincere veneration of Mary in her sorrows, the cause of her tears. As has been fittingly said: "The Tears of the Mother of Our Lord! Who could resist them? Not even He Who is the Creator of Life."

It is good to recall here that Our Lord, in this century, wanted devotion spread to the Sorrowful and Immaculate Heart of Mary. That was the mission of Berthe Petit, the Belgian mystic. It is obvious that all these varied missions of particular chosen souls in our times work together in a common thrust for the good and the peace of the world.

At Czestochowa, Poland, Saturday, June 18, 1983, Pope John Paul II said of the Sacred image of Our Lady there at the Jasna Gora Shrine, with a million people present, that the Black Madonna icon's eyes looked "tear-filled and sad".

APPENDIX D

Considering how Mary must sorrow over Cuba and our story of the Cuban exile in Louisiana with the weeping Fatima statues, the following is of interest.

Our Lady of Charity, Nuestra Señora de la Caridad del Cobre appeared in Cuba to three fishermen hundreds of years ago. In the past two months (this writing is of December, 1981) Our Lady of Charity seems to be appearing in Cuba again. This has been reported among Spanish speaking Cuban exiles in the United States. This news comes from Haiti by radio, Haiti being only about thirty miles away from Cuba. At this point the author cannot give any final confirmation but the reports seem authentic.

This time no boat, no fishermen are involved. Our Lady simply appears on the water offshore from Havana, suspended above it or moving about like Christ or Saint Peter on Lake Galilee. Unlike the original Nuestra Señora de la Caridad She is all in white, no blue. She has appeared with a Babe on her arms and with a crucifix.

In these apparitions Mary moves gently about, appears night and day and still appears at this writing. She has been seen by many people and this reminds us of the Cairo, Egypt apparitions. When the Cuban Communist authorities banned the people from the central Havana offshore area, people were able to see her from the sides of the area.

It is even said that the Communists fired a cannon or gun at the apparition. This reminds us of the Chinese Communists being fearful of the Lady who was the head of the Legion of Mary. And of the Polish high authorities, including a general, who opposed the removal of the International Pilgrim Virgin statue from the plane of the Blue Army at Warsaw a few years ago.

It is reported that Mary has given messages to a young girl, 15-16 years of age, who was persecuted by the Communists. The substance of Mary's message seems to be that if the Cuban people make enough penance and reparation Mary will return or give back Cuba to them. Also Mary said something to the effect that they should remember Her Name is Charity, but that they should not go off only with the name of charity, but should observe the meaning of the word charity.

The original shrine of Our Lady of Charity was at Santiago. It is interesting to note that the Cuban exile gentleman of the weeping Fatima statues in the New Orleans area expects to receive a statue of Our Lady of Charity shortly. It should involve an interesting development.

(Subsequent to this writing a report of the Cuba apparitions has appeared in *The Globe*, Dec. 29, 1981.)

APPENDIX E

Some persons ask how can Mary or Christ sorrow, "suffer" or weep when everyone in heaven is happy? That is a reasonable question and there is no easy answer. Perhaps some response can be attempted here.

First, in apparitions of angels or saints neither have bodies. The *persons*, however, angelic spirits or bodiless souls represent or present themselves, according to our limited abilities to receive communications, that is in "our language", in an apparitional "body" appearance.

Christ and Mary, however, do have their bodies and can communicate with men either bodily, by bilocation, or by some other mysterious way through human imagery so that we do know we are in contact with them whatever the means they employ. It is more than and different from a live TV image and communication.

Further, Jesus and Mary can show themselves in suffering (as Jesus in His Passion), sorrow and weeping without being really basically unhappy, and certainly without being unhappy in heaven. When Mary was once asked such a question Mary replied that she was happy in heaven but sorrowful on earth.

We might point out that a parent need not be unhappy deep down and can be at peace with God, while acting very sad or angry with a child needing correction. Similarly, we cannot actually say that God is "angry" as we are, but such is our language which He makes use of in communicating with His little children, as in the Bible. It is like dignified adults who use baby-talk with babies and "No, no!" and lifted finger signs with toddlers.

Another approach to the matter may be the following. Time in our world and in Eternity are not the same. "My ways are not your ways," says the Lord. Neither is our earthly and temporal space like the realms of the supernatural. Genuine mystics, as in ecstasy, transports, levitation and bilocation experience other than normal earthly dimensions.

While Christ suffered His Passion for us and Mary suffered for us long ago on earth, it is we who in our times are being redeemed *now* by Christ's sufferings and aided by Mary's when she stood then on Calvary, the Mother of Sorrows and was and is the Mediatrix of all graces. In this respect Christ and Mary might be considered as being at the center, the hub of a large, many spoked wheel. The spokes extend outwards through the centuries in many directions and through many enlarging rims.

We go back, as it were, through the spokes of contact to Christ and Mary then, nearly two thousand years ago, who were living then as they are living now. In some way we can experience now their sufferings then, as manifested today in apparitions. Of course, it is not all as simplistic as that. There are mysteries, however, and the facts remain, as attested by many saints and holy persons, that Christ and Mary have appeared and do appear in apparitions, sorrowing, suffering and weeping, at least as we see it, and in a "language" we understand.

The author does not intend to present any of the above concepts or illustrations as didactic truth, but as mere helpful speculations. But there can be no talk of improbability or impossibility in the presence of experienced facts. In a word when Christ and Mary appear to us, suffering, sorrowing, weeping, they are superior beings communicating from a supernatural world to earth-bound humans but in our language.

Syrian National Pilgrim Virgin weeping, Damascus

BIBLIOGRAPHY:

Arintero, O.P., Fr. John G., *The Mystical Evolution in the Development and Vitality of the Church,* 2 vols., tr. by Fr. Jordan Aumann, O.P., Tan Books and Publishers, Inc., Rockford, IL. (1978).

Anderson, Robin, *Saint Pius V,* St. Michael's Press (1973), Tan, (1978).

Aradi, Zsolt, *The Book of Miracles,* Farrar, Strauss and Cudahy, New York (1956).

Bandini, Rev. A. R., *The Miracle at Syracuse,* Academy Library Guild, Fresno, CA. (1956).

Bardi, Mons. Giuseppe, *St. Gemma Galgani,* tr. fr. Italian by Margherita M. Repton, St. Paul Edns., Boston (1951).

Benedict, Claire M., *Saint Sharbel, Mystic of the East,* The Ravengate Press, Cambridge, MA. (1977).

Bessières, S.J., Albert, *Wife, Mother and Mystic* (Bl. Anna Maria Taigi), tr. fr. French, Rev. Stephen Rigby, Tan (1970).

Biver, Comte Paul, *Père Lamy,* tr. fr. French, Msgr. John O'Connor with preface by Jacques Maritain, Tan (1973).

Boyer, Rev. A. A., *She Wears a Crown of Thorns,* (Marie Rose Ferron), Benziger, N.Y. (1946).

Breen, Stephen, *Recent Apparitions of the Blessed Virgin Mary,* Lumen Bks., J. S. Paluch Co., Chicago, IL. (1957).

Brewer, E. C., *A Dictionary of Miracles,* J. B. Lippincott Co., Republished by Gale Research Co., Book Tower, Detroit (1966).

Bruno, Clarice, *Roads to Padre Pio,* John Bruno Iberle, Chicago, IL. (1970).

Curley, Edmund F., *Battlefield Dropout, Life of St. Camillus,* Our Sunday Visitor Press, Huntington, IN. (1975).

Dahmus, Bede, *The Angels Our God Given Companions and Servants,* (Magdalen of the Cross — Mechtilde Schw--), tr. fr. German, Ave Maria Institute, Washington, N.J.

Delaney, John J., *Dictionary of Saints,* Doubleday & Co., Inc., Garden City, N.Y. (1980).

De Marchi, I.M.C., John, *The Immaculate Heart* (The True Story of Fatima), Farrar, Strauss and Young, N.Y. (1952).

Deutsch, Bernard F., *Our Lady of Ephesus,* Bruce Pub. Co., Milwaukee, WI. (1965).

Dupont, Yves, *Catholic Prophecy,* Tan (1970).

Eid, S. S., Chor-Bishop Joseph, *The Hermit of Lebanon, Blessed Sharbel,* St. Anthony of the Desert Church (Maronite), Fall River, MA. (rev. edn., 1965).

Fernandez, Emile E., T.O.Carm., *Nuestra Señora de la Caridad del Cobre (Our Lady of Charity, Patroness of Cuba),* Spanish and English version tr. fr. Sp. of League of Women of Cuban Cath. Action, Havana (1955); 3309 Yale Dr., Kenner, LA. 70082 (1982).

Flame of Love, Hungarian mother (bklt.), Immaculata-Verlag, 9000 St. Gallen, Switzerland (1977). (Mrs. L.F., 471 W-24th St., San Bernardino, CA. 92405).

Fox. Rev. Robert J., *Call of Heaven, Bro. Gino — Stigmatist,* Christendom Pubs., Front Royal, VA. (1982).

Garrigou-LaGrange, O.P., Rev. R., *The Three Ages of the Interior Life,* Vol. Two, tr. by Sr. M. Timothea Doyle, O.P., B. Herder Bk. Co., St. Louis, MO. (1948).

Gaudiose, Dorothy M., *Prophet of the People* (Padre Pio), Alba House, N.Y. (1974).

Gillet, H. M., *Famous Shrines of Our Lady,* Carroll Press, Westminster, MD. (1950).

Gobbi, Don Stefano, *Our Lady Speaks to Her Beloved Priests,* Marian Movement of Priests, 6th Am. edn., St. Charles Rectory, St. Francis, ME. (1980).

Haffert, John M., *Explosion of the Supernatural,* AMI Press, Washington, N.J. (1975).

Handbook on Guadalupe, Franciscan Marytown Press, Kenosha, WI. (1974).

Harvey, Lawrence F., *By the Queen's Command,* John S. Burns and Sons, Glasgow (1952).

Hogan, S.J., Rev. J. A., *The Pilgrimage of Our Lady of Prompt Succor,* Society of St. Ursula, New Orleans, LA. (1907).

Imbert-Goubeyre, Dr., *La Stigmatisation et L'Extase Divine,* 2 vols Amat (1894).

Johnston, Francis, *When Millions Saw Mary,* Augustine Pub. Co., Chulmleigh, Devon, United Kingdom (bklt. — 1980).

Johnston, Francis, *Alexandrina, The Agony and the Glory,* Veritas Pubs., Dublin (1979); Tan, (1982).

Jongen, S.M.M., H., *Look — the Madonna Is Weeping,* tr. fr. French, Montfort Pubs., Bay Shore, N.Y. (1959).

Lamarche, Rev. J. A., *The Road That Leads to Life . . .* (Gaby's Diary), St. Raphael Edns., Sherbrooke, P.Q., Canada (1974).

Lambertini, A Cura Di Gabriella, *Segno Dei Tempi?*, Magalina Editrice, Brescia, via Cavaletto 25 (II Edisione — 1974).

Marguerite, *Message of Merciful Love to Little Souls,* POPE Pubs., Box 6161, San Rafael, CA. (Am. edn. — 1979).

Mary of Agreda, *Mystical City of God,* (1670) 4 vols., AMI Press, Washington, N.J.

Miceli, S.J., Vincent P., *The Antichrist,* Christopher Publishing House, West Hanover, MA. (1981).

McGrath, P.A., Rt. Rev. Wm. C., *Fatima or World Suicide,* Scarboro Bluffs, Ontario, Canada (1950).

Monden, S.J., Louis, *Signs and Wonders,* Desclee Co., N.Y. (1966).

Mother Marie St. Cecile of Rome, *A Canadian Mystic of Our Day,* (Dina Bélanger), based on the French of *Une Vie dans le Christ* of Dom Leonce Crenier, O.S.B., by Mary St. Cuthebert, R.J.M., Sillery, Quebec, Canada (1946).

Osee, John, *Call of the Virgin at San Damiano,* The Christopher Pub. House, North Quincy, MA. (1977).

Philipon, O.P., M. M., *Conchita,* Alba House, N.Y. (1978).

Palmer, O.S.B., Jerome, *Our Lady Returns to Egypt,* Culligan Pubs., San Bernardino, CA. (1969).

Plea through a Professed Sister, *Our Lady of America,* (personal diary, 1971, with supplement), New Riegel, OH.

Poulain, S.J., A., *Graces of Interior Prayer,* 1st Eng. edn., 1910; reprint, Celtic Cross Books, Westminster, VT. (1978).

Quatman, D. E., *Panaya Kapulu, House of Our Lady,* American Soc. of Ephesus, Lima, OH. (1960).

Rahner, S.J., Karl, *Visions and Prophecies,* Herder and Herder, N.Y. (1963).

Reparation Soc. of the Immaculate Heart of Mary, Inc., John Ryan, S.J., Foreword, *The Great Flaming Furnace of the Sacred Heart,* Fatima House, Baltimore, MD. (1976).

Roberdel, Pierre, *Prophecies of La Fraudais,* Edns. Resiac, 53150 Montsours, France (Les Editions Saint-Raphael, Inc., Sherbrooke, Quebec, Canada — 1977).

Roschini, O.S.M., P. Gabriel M., *Teresa Musco,* 1943-1976, *"Crocifissa col Crocifisso",* Instituto Anselmi, Marigliano (Na) Italy.

Sanchez, Rev. Benjamin Martin, *The Last Times,* Opus Reginaè Sacratissimi Rosarii.

Schug, Cap., John A., *Padre Pio,* Our Sunday Visitor Press, Huntington, IN. (1976).

Sister Faustina, Apostle of Divine Mercy, tr. fr. French of Dr. H. W., Mercy of God Apostolate, Marian Fathers, Stockbridge, MA.

Sister Josefa Menendez, *The Way of Divine Love,* Tan (1972).

Sorrowful and Immaculate Heart of Mary, (Messages of Berthe Petit, Franciscan Tertiary), tr. fr. French by a nun of Kylemore Abbey, Franciscan Martytown Press, Kenosha, WI. (1966).

Spadafora, Rt. Rev. Francesco, *The Incredible Life Story of Sister Elena Aiello* (The Calabrian Holy Nun), tr. fr. Italian by Rt. Rev. Angelo R. Cioffi, Theo Gaus, Inc., Brooklyn, N.Y. (1964).

Steiner, Johannes, *Therese Neumann,* (orig. *Theres Neumann von Konnersreuth* at München) Alba House, Staten Island, N.Y. (1967).

Van Speybrouck, Edward, *The Very Rev. Father Paul of Moll,* tr. fr. French by a member of the Order of St. Benedict, Tan (1977).

Viti, Canon Paolo, *The Queen of Heaven to Her Beloved Priests,* tr. fr. Italian by Fr. Charles D. Gorman, Gateway Press, St. Louis, MO. (flat, offset edn. — 1973).

Vogl, Adalbert, *Therese Neumann, A Living Stigmatist.* Valley Press. San Jose, CA. (1956).

Wilson, Jan, *The Shroud of Turin,* Doubleday & Co., Inc., Garden City, N.Y. (1978)

Zaki, Pearl, *Our Lord's Mother Visits Egypt in 1968,* Day El Alam, El Arabi. (Obtainable at Community of St. Mary's — below)

Zaremba, O.F.M., Rev. Theodore, *Mercy is Forever* (Sr. Faustina & Mercy of God devotion), Franciscan Publishers, Pulaski, WI. (1957).

Hafouri, Msgr. Dr. Georges — see articles, 1981 issues *Stella Maris,* Edns. Du Parvis / Parvis-Verlag CH-1631 Hauteville, re Damascus Syrian Pilgrim Virgin Fatima statue weepings. *Stella Maris,* 16 Octobre 1981 also lists a number of works on apparitions, seers, stigmatists, etc. Some concern persons not mentioned in this book. (Hauteville/Bulle, Suisse)

Tangen, Rev. Ronald, tapes on Bro. Gino, O.B.L. Victory Mission, Inc., R.R. 2, Box 25, Brookings, South Dakota, 57006.

Helpful Catholic organs:

Catholic Commentator, Interview, Louis Kaczmarek, Feb. 27, 1980, Baton Rouge, LA.

Clarion Herald, New Orleans, LA. Issues, July, August, 1972.

Divine Love, P. O. Box 24, Fresno, CA. 93707, "Prophetic Warnings" issue No. 86, 1981 (Sister Elena Aiello).

Immaculata magazine, 1600 West Park Ave., Libertyville, IL. 60048.

Queen magazine, Montfort Fathers, Bay Shore, N.Y.